Spiritual Deliverance Training for Personal and Team Ministry

POWER to DELIVER
MINISTRY MANUAL

STEPHEN BEAUCHAMP

FORERUNNER PUBLISHING
KANSAS CITY, MISSOURI

Power to Deliver Ministry Manual—Spiritual Deliverance Training for Personal and Team Ministry
by Stephen Beauchamp

Published by Forerunner Publishing
International House of Prayer
3535 E. Red Bridge Road
Kansas City, Missouri 64137
ihopkc.org/books

© Copyright 2019 by Forerunner Publishing
All rights reserved. Published 2019

This book or any parts of this book may not be reproduced in any form, stored in a retrieval system, or transmitted in any form by any means—electronic, mechanical, photocopy, recording, or otherwise—without prior written permission of the publisher, except as provided by United States of America copyright law.

Forerunner Publishing is the book-publishing division of the International House of Prayer of Kansas City, an evangelical missions organization that exists to partner in the Great Commission by advancing 24/7 prayer and proclaiming the beauty of Jesus and His glorious return.

ISBN: 978-1-938060-46-5

Unless otherwise noted, all Scripture quotations taken from the New American Standard Bible® (NASB), Copyright © 1960, 1962, 1963, 1968, 1971, 1972, 1973, 1975, 1977, 1995 by The Lockman Foundation. Used by permission. www.Lockman.org. Scripture quotations marked (NKJV) are taken from the New King James Version®. Copyright © 1982 by Thomas Nelson. Used by permission. All rights reserved. Scripture quotations marked (KJV) are taken from the King James Bible. Public domain.

All emphasis in Scripture quotations is the author's.

Cover design by Emily Flinn
Interior design by Emily Flinn and Dale Jimmo
Author photo by Madison Pierce

Printed in the United States of America

28 27 26 25 24 23 22 21 20 19 18   1 2 3 4 5 6 7 8 9

Contents

Acknowledgments | 1
Preface | 3

1. **Understanding Demonic Influence and Spiritual Deliverance | 5**
   Demonic Access and Influence 5
   Three Levels of Demonic Influence 6
   Spiritual Authority 7
   Defining a Stronghold 9
   Breaking Strongholds 9
   Inner Healing 10
   Forgiveness 11
   Soul Ties 12
   Generational Assignments 13

2. **Developing a Deliverance Ministry | 15**
   Deliverance Team Roles and Responsibilities 15
   Team Selection 16
   Team Etiquette and Procedure 16
   Qualifications for Those Seeking Deliverance Ministry 17
   Questionnaire and Interview 18
   Post-ministry 19

3. **Deliverance Procedures: Steps for Personal, Level One, and Level Two Deliverance Sessions | 21**
   Personal Deliverance: Six Steps to Break Cycles of Demonic Influence 21
   Level One Deliverance: Five-Step Procedure for Individual Ministry 24
   Level Two Deliverance: Ten-Step Procedure for Team Ministry 26
   Maintaining Freedom 28

4. **Spiritual Deliverance Prayers | 31**
   Prayer of Submission to the Lordship of Jesus Christ 31
   Prayer to Break Soul Ties 31
   Prayer to Break Generational Assignments and Demonic Curses 32
   Prayer to Break the Power of Witchcraft 32
   Prayer to Break Strongholds 33
   Prayer of Blessing 34

5. **The Sixteen Strongholds | 35**
    Stronghold of Antichrist 36
    Stronghold of Bondage 37
    Stronghold of a Deaf and Dumb Spirit 38
    Stronghold of Death 39
    Stronghold of Divination 40
    Stronghold of Error 42
    Stronghold of Fear 43
    Stronghold of Harlotry 44
    Stronghold of Haughtiness 45
    Stronghold of Heaviness 46
    Stronghold of Infirmity 47
    Stronghold of Jealousy 48
    Stronghold of Lying 49
    Stronghold of Perversion 50
    Stronghold of a Seducing Spirit 52
    Stronghold of Stupor 53

Appendix 1: Pre- and Post-ministry Forms | 55
    Deliverance Ministry Questionnaire 57
    Release and Waiver SAMPLE 73
    Deliverance Session Report 75
    Deliverance Ministry Feedback 77

Appendix 2: Pre- and Post-ministry Handouts | 79
    Preparation for Receiving Deliverance 80
    Forgiveness 81
    Moving Forward after Deliverance 82

Appendix 3: Prayer for Release from Freemasonry | 83

Acknowledgments

Over the years I have been blessed to be acquainted with some of the most anointed leaders in spiritual deliverance ministry.

I would like to thank Teresa Castleman who was the head of deliverance ministry at the Brownsville Assembly of God during the time of an historic revival. She was the first to train me in this ministry, and her insight and discernment laid a solid foundation for me as young man who felt called to deliverance ministry.

I would also like to thank the various teachers, such as Dr. Michael Brown, Bob Gladstone, Mike Bickle, Pablo Bottari, Carlos Annacondia, David Hogan, and Bill Sudduth, whose messages, books, and ministries have helped equip me along the way.

I would like to thank Allen Hood, my dear friend and assistant director of the International House of Prayer of Kansas City, who asked me to build and lead the deliverance ministry of IHOPKC. His encouragement for me to step into a place of leadership was a significant factor leading to the development of this resource.

This manual would not have been produced without the many prayers and service of all the IHOPKC deliverance team members who stayed faithful to the call to love the broken and commit to seeing freedom come to those who are oppressed.

My thanks to you all.

Preface

It has always been a desire of mine to create a step-by-step, user-friendly spiritual deliverance manual for those in need of help ministering in this area. When we read the various instances of demonic deliverance in the Bible, we are often left without details to guide us concerning the process or context in which these events occurred, leaving us with many questions and opinions about how things should be done in our day and time. As a result, there have been various approaches to deliverance ministry that have taken us outside the parameters of the Word of God or have led to it being conducted in an unhealthy and, sometimes, abusive manner.

Over the years of ministering in deliverance, I have seen the common occurrence of well-meaning ministers disregarding the dignity of those who were living under the influence of demonic forces and exposing their personal issues in an inconsiderate and public manner. It was out of zeal, personal mistakes, and lack of lasting fruit that I began to seek the Lord for insight concerning an effective way to operate in deliverance ministry.

Through a sound, biblical foundation, specific and direct prayers, and with proven, effective tools, the function of this manual is to provide a clear, concise way to build a personal ministry team, help you determine who qualifies for this type of ministry, and walk you through a succinct process of confronting demonic influence in the life of the recipient. It includes tools that I have gathered from various approaches, biblical studies, and personal revelations to produce a fruitful, healthy, and simple way to help people with their spiritual needs.

This deliverance ministry manual primarily emphasizes how to deal with spiritual influences. Every individual should continue to search for increased insight and growth in order to navigate the various complexities that arise within the subjects of spiritual warfare and mental, physical, and emotional health. While this manual is thorough concerning the issue of spiritual deliverance, it is not exhaustive in other areas of healing and restoration for the individual, such as inner healing, counseling, and discipleship. I highly recommend researching the various approaches to inner healing, physical healing, counseling, and spiritual freedom for the sake of a well-balanced approach to these often situationally complicated issues.

My goal with this manual is to train as many as possible on how to partner with the Lord in this holy, much-needed, oftentimes-neglected ministry. This manual is not to be used in psychological manipulation through accusation and suggestion, but rather as a tool in cooperation with the leading of the Holy Spirit. Additionally, this manual should not be used in a rigid, methodical manner void of the life of God's presence.

As the power of the Holy Spirit is increasingly manifested on the earth, we will continue to see a great need for training in dealing with demonic strongholds. I believe God will use this resource to equip many in the fulfillment of the Isaiah 61:1 ministry to set the captives free. As the world around us continues to pursue the works of darkness and participate in behavior that opens their lives to that darkness, we, as the Body of Jesus Christ, will continue to find ourselves used by the Lord as a source where people can find true freedom.

For a complete understanding of my personal views, as well as my suggestion on where to begin in the area of deliverance ministry, I suggest pairing this manual with my book, *Power to Deliver: A Guide to Spiritual Warfare and Freedom* (Shippensburg, PA: Destiny Image, 2015). In it you will find a practical and theological explanation of my biblical interpretation concerning spiritual warfare and spiritual deliverance ministry. The book also serves as a solid foundation before launching into ministry with this manual.

Stephen Beauchamp

Understanding Demonic Influence and Spiritual Deliverance

DEMONIC ACCESS AND INFLUENCE

There are several ways that a demonic spirit can gain access and control in the life of a person. The reality of demonic activity is quite obvious once you begin addressing the areas in a person's life where they are experiencing difficulty obeying God's Word. A popular question asked in deliverance ministry is, "Can a born-again Christian have a demon?" When someone gets saved or is born again, their spirit is renewed by the Holy Spirit of God. However, the body and soul are still under the influence of the fall of man. It is very important to note that although there is a distinction between body, soul, and spirit, the three are very much connected and can influence one another; for example, sinning in the body will affect you spiritually.

> *Now may the God of peace Himself sanctify you entirely; and may your spirit and soul and body be preserved complete, without blame at the coming of our Lord Jesus Christ.* (1 Thessalonians 5:23)

If spiritual deliverance were solely based on the regeneration of the human spirit, then we would have no need for deliverance ministry, but rather just the need to lead a person to salvation. Whether an unclean spirit is in, on, or around a person doesn't really matter. (We do consistently see born again believers needing deliverance from various internal spiritual influences.) Not everyone who becomes born again automatically gets free from emotional wounding or mental strongholds. Even after a person's spirit is born again, the enemy seeks through temptation to draw them into sinful behavior resulting in the development of strongholds.

Mind: the main battleground where lies are conceived and believed
Will: the place of choice where the sin is completed (leading to responses in the emotions and body)
Emotions: the place where feelings and responses are felt (from the demonic influence of lies in the mind)

The Greek word for spirit is *pneuma*, which means "breath" or "wind." Just like the wind, demonic spirits cannot be seen but can indeed be felt or discerned through their effects. Because we do not always see how a spirit is influencing someone, it is helpful to know some of the most common ways the demonic gains access (this is not an exhaustive list):

1. Trauma (tragic events)
    a. Physical abuse
    b. Sexual abuse
    c. Verbal abuse
    d. Psychological abuse
    e. Spiritual abuse
    f. Accidents and near-death experiences
    g. Fearful encounters (shock)

2. The five senses (gates to the soul)
    a. Sinfully viewing wickedness
    b. Sinfully listening to demonically influenced music
    c. Speaking curses over yourself or others
    d. Physically acting out sin in any way

3. Deception
    a. Accusations about yourself and others
    b. Doctrinal error or false religions (false teachings about Christ)
    c. Every form of occult practice

4. Generational sin and curses
    a. Familiar patterns of sin throughout one's family line
    b. Demonic curses invoked upon one's life and family

THREE LEVELS OF DEMONIC INFLUENCE

Level One: Oppression

The first level of demonic influence is the most common among believers. Being a Christian means that we are part of a spiritual conflict or war, and we must realize that we will experience demonic resistance as we try to obey God on the earth. Every Christian experiences warfare and must learn to equip themselves with the Word and Spirit of God in order to resist and gain victory over demonic attacks. In most cases, people who think they are in need of deliverance ministry simply have not applied their God-given authority to their own situation.

Oppression involves greater demonic influence than just being tempted. Temptation is not a sin. This level is reached when the person has fallen into agreement with the lies of the enemy. It is usually a lack of spiritual discipline that gives a demon the ability to oppress a believer and control their lives. This person can wholeheartedly be a believing Christian and is able to pray, worship, and read the Word of God; however, they have succumbed to the attack from the enemy (physically, mentally, emotionally, etc.) and are now in need of a form of deliverance. In most cases, this person simply needs someone to come alongside them and walk them through repentance, forgiveness, and renouncing the lies they have agreed with, lies that the enemy is now using to oppress them. (See page 106–107 of *Power to Deliver*.[1])

Level Two: Torment

The tormented person is under such demonic influence that they may not be able to pray, worship, or read the Word of God. In most cases of torment, the person has experienced some deep form of spiritual, physical, verbal, or emotional trauma and is in need of the prayer and ministry of others in order for the strongholds to be broken. The enemy has gained access and established control to such a degree that thorough deliverance ministry, pastoral support, and restoration through discipleship is needed.

During deliverance prayer, this person might go into a physical, demonic manifestation—in other words, screaming, crying, choking, going unconscious, slithering, growling, etc. However, these manifestations do not have to occur in each situation, and when the ministry is done properly, as this manual will teach you, violent or disruptive manifestations rarely occur.

Level Three: Domination

The person under the third level of demonic influence has never accepted Jesus as Lord and Savior, and the enemy is in total domination of their mind. This level of bondage occurs when a person willfully requests that the demons enter their life and take control (this includes all forms of occult practices, false religions, etc.). It also occurs when a person experiences severe emotional pain and is unable to cope under that pain (sometimes resulting in conditions such as mental illness, dissociative identity disorder, etc.).

Most people who are dominated in the United States can be found in mental institutions or penitentiaries, but could be more integrated in society depending on the country in which you live. Do not attempt to administer deliverance to a dominated person without a clear confirmation from the Lord. In most cases the person will not receive ministry and may try to manipulate you and your team. Ministry to this level needs to be the result of a divine appointment, where this situation is brought to you through divine encounter and the leading of the Holy Spirit, rather than you seeking it out. (For more detail on the three levels of demonic influence, see pages 106–111 of *Power to Deliver*.)

SPIRITUAL AUTHORITY

The life and ministry of Jesus clearly showed the authority the children of God have over demonic powers. The same authority operates through us today, and we must have confidence in that authority. While the enemy has been defeated, his ability to deceive has not changed. Spiritual deliverance is a matter of confronting places of deception with the truth.

> *"Behold, I give you the authority to trample on serpents and scorpions, and over all the power of the enemy, and nothing shall by any means hurt you."* (Luke 10:19)

> *"And you shall know the truth, and the truth shall make you free."* (John 8:32 NKJV)

When a person experiences a spiritual attack in their personal life, their family, their physical body, or their home, that person has every right to speak directly to whatever spirit is trying to influence them. It is not necessary to get the name of a spirit in order to command it to leave; however, the Holy Spirit could reveal to you through the gift of discerning of spirits exactly what type of spirit is involved. The very nature of Satan and his demons is to lie; therefore, trying to communicate with evil spirits is neither wise nor necessary.

> *"He was a murderer from the beginning, and does not stand in the truth because there is no truth in him. Whenever he speaks a lie, he speaks from his own nature, for he is a liar and the father of lies."* (John 8:44)

If during a time of deliverance ministry a spirit begins to manifest, command that spirit to be silent and make sure the individual has truly repented and renounced any agreement with that spirit. Never allow a spirit to manipulate the session or cause harm or trauma to the person. Simply take authority over the spirit in the name of Jesus, commanding it to be silent and to stop manifesting. When a spirit has the ability to manifest through a person it is a clear sign that the person is still in agreement with that spirit's ability to do so. The only way a spirit can speak through a person or physically control them is if that person is yielding to its deception over their life. If this occurs, go back to the initial steps* of the session in order to remove any hidden agreements a person might have with the unclean spirits. (*These are repentance, forgiveness, and renouncing, using the *Prayer of Submission to the Lordship of Jesus Christ*. This occurs in step 2 during Level One deliverance or step 3 during Level Two deliverance.)

Due to the amount of sinful behavior taking place on the earth, commanding a spirit to go to certain places such as "dry places," "the pit of hell," or "the cross" is unnecessary and unbiblical. If it were possible, Jesus and the disciples would have commanded spirits never to return. However, Jesus actually warns people of the reality of a spirit's ability to return.

> *"Now when the unclean spirit goes out of a man, it passes through waterless places seeking rest, and does not find it. Then it says, 'I will return to my house from which I came'."* (Matthew 12:43–44)

When confronting darkness within a person's life or home, make sure that person is in agreement with you. Confronting disembodied spirits without the direct leading of God or the agreement of the person in authority over that domain could be a waste of time and energy, especially if the person or people within that home, territory, or region aren't willing to submit to the lordship of Jesus Christ.

No one has more authority over children than the parents. When a child is in need of deliverance, the most effective way for a minister to help that child gain and maintain their freedom is to train the parents how to take authority in the realm of the spirit over their home and family. It is imperative to train parents how to operate in the God-given authority they have to pray over their children. Parents should not be dependent on another person to pray deliverance over their children. If the parents are unaware of that authority, then the child's potential to become demonically influenced again after the deliverance is much greater.

All believers are called to cast out demons. Some will have the assignment in a more full-time way, but we are all called to set the captives free.

> *"And as you go, preach, saying, 'The kingdom of heaven is at hand.' Heal the sick, raise the dead, cleanse the lepers, cast out demons. Freely you have received, freely give."* (Matthew 10:7–8 NKJV)

> *The Spirit of the Lord God is upon me, because the Lord has anointed me to bring good news to the afflicted; He has sent me to bind up the brokenhearted, to proclaim liberty to captives and freedom to prisoners.* (Isaiah 61:1)

(For more on this subject, see chapter 6 in *Power to Deliver*.)

DEFINING A STRONGHOLD

There are different perspectives concerning what and where strongholds are. However, it is clear that the only reference in the New Testament to strongholds is an analogy Paul the apostle uses to address belief patterns formed in the mind. The way those strongholds are broken is through proclamation of the truth and continued obedience to that truth.

> *For though we walk in the flesh, we do not war according to the flesh, for the weapons of our warfare are not of the flesh, but divinely powerful for the destruction of fortresses [strongholds]. We are destroying speculations and every lofty thing raised up against the knowledge of God, and we are taking every thought captive to the obedience of Christ.* (2 Corinthians 10:3–5)

Strongholds are the construct of demonic influence after a person has given the enemy a place in his or her life through sin. Once demons have gained access to our lives, they begin to systematically go after our mind, will, and emotions. Although all three elements of the soul are equally susceptible to demonic influence, I have found that the mind is often the first target, as well as the primary battleground. When the enemy is mounting an attack, lies based on our experiences begin to dominate and reshape our thought life. Next, our will and emotions become involved and fall before the onslaught. We choose to believe the lies and then act or react accordingly, damaging our hearts through sin. This process constitutes a stronghold. Simply put, a stronghold exists when a demonic spirit has the ability to consistently speak a lie and provoke a negative or sinful behavioral response in us (*Power to Deliver*, 99).

This manual addresses specific strongholds that have been formed by an individual's experiences or partnership with demonic spirits. The strongholds mentioned in this manual are not an exhaustive list, nor are they to be referenced as demons themselves. From a theological standpoint, there are a multitude of potential strongholds that could be mentioned, with various names and titles from the numerous languages on the earth. In the manual you will find sixteen different strongholds and the behaviors associated with them—these have been mentioned for the sake of identifying potential areas where a demonic spirit has a stronghold.

Deliverance isn't just a power encounter—it is a truth encounter.

BREAKING STRONGHOLDS

This manual's foundational approach to deliverance ministry is to take a person at any level of demonic influence through a structured time of prayer, as part of which that person goes through a process of breaking all agreement with any particular spirit associated with certain habitual behavior, or "strongholds." The strongholds can be identified through the information gathered in the ministry questionnaire (available in the appendix) and interview that take place prior to deliverance ministry. In order to avoid any psychological damage, it is crucial that this approach is thoroughly explained to the ministry recipient before the prayer time begins.

Here are the most imperative points to explain clearly:

1. This time of prayer is something the team is doing **with** the individual, not *to* them.
2. The team is addressing the spiritual realm and the demonic, not the individual person.
3. Not every stronghold or behavior being prayed about is necessarily an issue present in the recipient's life. All strongholds in the manual are being covered for the sake of being thorough. (The team should not assume that all strongholds have been identified through the interview and questionnaire, and should be thorough during the prayer time.)
4. A demonic attack is an *occasional* occurrence; a stronghold is characterized by the *consistent occurrence* of behaviors and thought patterns. Although a person may have fallen into a behavior from time to time, it does not mean it is a fully formed stronghold of the enemy. A stronghold is something that consistently controls a person.

Once the ministry time has been clearly explained and agreed upon, the team leader can begin leading the prayer time, which will include addressing the sixteen strongholds. Chapter 3, *Deliverance Procedures*, gives the structure for the prayer time, and chapters 4–5 provide specific prayers to use and the listing of sixteen demonic strongholds and associated behaviors.

Prayer to break a stronghold consists of the team leader walking a person through repenting of any sin associated with that stronghold, followed by renouncing any agreement or participation with a spirit or behavior associated with that stronghold. This prayer time continues until all behavioral manifestations of a stronghold have been renounced. The process can be repeated as many times as needed if the individual or the team feels it is necessary. This prayer time should not be done in an overly methodical manner void of the presence of the Holy Spirit. Take your time and make sure the person you are praying with is fully aware and understands what they are doing with sincerity. Communication between the team and the individual is very important. Do not move on to another stronghold until all members in the room (team members and ministry recipient) feel the release to do so.

INNER HEALING

It cannot be emphasized enough that you cannot separate spiritual deliverance from inner or emotional healing. They are experiences that work hand in hand, one affecting the strength or influence of the other. We fall into error when we neglect to address wounded emotions during the spiritual deliverance process, just as much as it is error to simply counsel or attempt emotional healing without awareness of the spiritual influences that have contributed to the emotional pain or trauma.

Our negative relational experiences with leaders, parents, siblings, spouses, and loved ones produce a distorted view of God and ourselves, leaving us in need of emotional restoration. A large part of that restoration will come from establishing the truths of God being a good Father/parental figure who can be trusted, Jesus being a humble King who relates to us passionately as His Bride, and the Holy Spirit being a perfect helper who comforts us throughout our lives in a fallen world. The truth of who God is and how He feels about us can, and will, bring emotional healing. Therefore, we must take the time to minister those truths.

As you are walking a person through this manual and its prayers, you will need an awareness of when to minister to the emotions of the recipient. The team members, along with the ministry of the Holy Spirit, will help recognize the moments when it is time to apply your inner healing training or tools. Even with the enemy removed, the ministry recipient will have wounds that need healing. If we do not help the mind and emotions recover, then demonic spirits will return at a later date and establish new strongholds. For this reason I believe inner healing needs to be incorporated into the general philosophy of deliverance. I am not going to address the subject of inner healing in this manual, but I strongly encourage you to pursue training and experience in this area before you embark on deliverance ministry (*Power to Deliver,* 127).

FORGIVENESS

Unforgiveness is one of the most significant issues to address before entering into any type of deliverance. The principle in Matthew 18:34 clearly relates the enemy's torment to a person's inability to forgive.

> *"And his lord, moved with anger, handed him over to the torturers until he should repay all that was owed him. My heavenly Father will also do the same to you, if each of you does not forgive his brother from your heart."* (Matthew 18:34–35)

> *"For if you forgive men their trespasses, your heavenly Father will also forgive you. But if you do not forgive their trespasses, neither will your Father forgive your trespasses."* (Matthew 6:14–15 NKJV)

A time of deep reflection and heart searching may be necessary due to the tendency people have to bury areas of hurt or pain resulting from the way another person has mistreated them. Take your time with this stage of the deliverance process. If a person is unable to find the ability to forgive then do not proceed with deliverance ministry, but continue counseling him or her in hopes of bringing them to a willingness to forgive. Giving a proper understanding of what forgiveness truly is can aid in this.

What Forgiveness Is Not
- Forgiveness is not saying that what a person did to you is okay. It is not okay. It will never be okay. It was wrong.
- Forgiveness is not a feeling. It is obedience to God's Word. It is a choice. It is a decision to obey God.
- Forgiveness is not healing. Forgiveness paves the way or opens the door for healing. If you have forgiven someone and still feel pain, it's because you need to receive your healing. The forgiveness comes first, then the healing.

What Forgiveness Is
- Forgiveness is a command. One of the biggest mistakes we could ever make is thinking forgiveness is an option. It is not an option; it is a commandment. Forgiveness is releasing the offender to God; it is turning them over to God.

Effective Steps to Forgiving Others
1. Get alone and ask the Lord to show you the people you need to forgive.
2. Write down the names of people you need to forgive. (They may be from seemingly insignificant incidents, or from the recent past or long ago, like the little girl from the third grade, your fifth-grade schoolteacher, etc.)

3. Include yourself (if applicable).
4. Include any angry feelings toward God (if applicable).
5. Go over each name with the Lord and express to Him how they have hurt you.
6. Write down what they did and why you need to forgive them.
7. List whatever feelings you had and the degree to which you felt them. (Example: "I was so angry, I did not care if they fell and hurt themselves—actually, I wish they had." "I wished I could have died because of the humiliation.")
8. Choose to forgive and release them. "Lord, I choose to forgive and release [*name of person*]."
9. Do it. Say, "I forgive them."
10. Write a letter to each person. "I forgive and release you from . . ." (This step is optional. Not all letters will be sent. These are an act of faith. The Lord will see your sincerity.)
11. Look at yourself in the mirror, and forgive and release yourself from everything that you need to forgive yourself for. Declare to yourself that you are forgiven.
12. Receive and believe that you are forgiven by God. (When ministering to others, look the person in the eyes and declare to them, "You are forgiven.")

SOUL TIES

Although you cannot find the term *soul tie* in Scripture, you will find words that support the concept, such as *knit* and *cleave*.

Knit: to link firmly or closely; to cause to grow together. [2]

Cleave: to adhere strongly to; to be come very strongly attached to or emotionally involved with. [3]

There can be emotional connections within our soul that can be good and healthy or connections that are negative and can lead to ungodliness.

Examples of Good / Godly Soul Ties

Therefore shall a man leave his father and his mother, and shall cleave unto his wife: and they shall be one flesh. (Genesis 2:24 KJV)

The soul of Jonathan was knit to the soul of David, and Jonathan loved him as his own soul. (1 Samuel 18:1 NKJV)

Examples of Bad / Ungodly Soul Ties

Or do you not know that he who is joined to a harlot is one body with her? For "the two," He says, "shall become one flesh." (1 Corinthians 6:16)

And Dinah the daughter of Leah, which she bare unto Jacob, went out to see the daughters of the land. And when Shechem the son of Hamor the Hivite, prince of the country, saw her, he took her, and lay with her, and defiled her. And his soul clave unto Dinah the daughter of Jacob." (Genesis 34:1–3 KJV)

An ungodly connection (soul tie) is created whenever someone commits sexual immorality with another individual. Therefore every ungodly sexual experience outside of a marriage covenant must be addressed. Each union was an emotional, physical, and spiritual transaction. The result can be lingering memories that produce regret, shame, anger, disappointment, or even unholy desires.

Another way soul ties can affect us is through articles of affection, such as a gift from a former relationship (a picture, a ring, a jacket, etc.). Negative or sinful memories that continually torment an individual could be the result of a lingering spiritual connection or soul tie that the enemy is using.

GENERATIONAL ASSIGNMENTS

It is important to distinguish between demonic generational assignments and Deuteronomic curses. According to the law of Moses, God promises to visit the iniquity of the fathers on the children down to the third and fourth generations (Deuteronomy 5:9). This law still stands for unbelievers, but if you are a believer you are no longer under the law. God is not holding you accountable for the sins of your parents and grandparents. Jesus became a curse for you when He hung on the cross so you would no longer bear the curse of God (Galatians 3:13). This is why the Holy Spirit does not convict you of sins committed by your family members and those in your bloodline (*Power to Deliver*, 98).

> *"Keeping mercy for thousands, forgiving iniquity and transgression and sin, by no means clearing the guilty, visiting [punishing] the iniquity of the fathers upon the children and upon the children's children to the third and to the fourth generation."*
> (Exodus 34:7 NKJV)

> *Our fathers sinned, and are no more; it is we who have borne [been punished for] their iniquities.* (Lamentations 5:7)

These verses still apply to those who have not received Jesus as their Lord and Savior. However, Jesus Christ has redeemed us from the curse of the law. If you have received Jesus as your Lord and Savior, the application of generational curses due to the sins of your family has been broken. The spiritual bondages that have been passed down from generation to generation no longer have a right to continue in your life.

> *Christ redeemed us from the curse of the law, having become a curse for us—for it is written, "Cursed is everyone who hangs on a tree."* (Galatians 3:13)

Although the curse does not apply to those who are born again, there remains a need to address those demonic spirits that would try to perpetuate the sinful behavior in the person's life and following generations. When particular patterns of sin or sickness become evident within a person's family line, it can be the result of a generational familiar spirit. These spirits are often ones that have been associated with the previous sins committed by the ancestors. Many false religions and occult practices curse individuals with these generational assignments upon initiation, and it is these curses/assignments that this manual addresses and that must be broken.

Curses that have been attached to a family line on the basis of agreement with darkness must be repented of and renounced accordingly. Demonic generational curses can absolutely be active in the life of a believer. Anyone who may have family members who are involved in the occult or false religions can be subject to the effect of vows and curses those family members have agreed with. These spirits still need to be addressed, broken, and cast out.

Notes

[1] Stephen Beauchamp, *Power to Deliver: A Guide to Spiritual Warfare and Freedom* (Shippensburg, PA: Destiny Image, 2015).

[2] "Knit." Merriam-Webster.com. Accessed October 20, 2018. https://www.merriam-webster.com/dictionary/knit.

[3] *Oxford Dictionaries Online*. S.v. "cleave." Accessed October 20, 2018, https://en.oxforddictionaries.com.

Developing a Deliverance Ministry

There are different approaches to deliverance ministry, each with its own process. These approaches vary depending on the level of deliverance that is necessary. Personal deliverance is between the Lord and the individual (see "Personal Deliverance: Six Steps to Break Cycles of Demonic Influence" in chapter 3). If a person is unable to obtain freedom on his or her own, or with the help of an individual minister (see "Level One Deliverance: Five-Step Procedure for Individual Ministry" in chapter 3), then team deliverance ministry may be needed. It is never wise for a single minister to attempt Level Two deliverance on another person. A team approach will help ensure safety, confidentiality, and accountability and help avoid liability and unfounded accusation. In team deliverance ministry a trained team, consisting of two to three members, facilitates prayer addressing the needs of the individual. Refer to the chapter 1 discussion of levels of demonic influence in order to discern whether a person needs team deliverance or can do it on their own.

DELIVERANCE TEAM ROLES AND RESPONSIBILITIES

A deliverance team usually has three members. There may be times when you are unable to have all three positions present and will need to hold the sessions with only two people. During these times, it is best to have the second person both observe and intercede while staying focused on the recipient. I highly recommend never operating in deliverance ministry alone. This will also protect you from potential accusations against you or your ministry.

Leader
The team leader is in charge of the deliverance session. This person should be properly trained and have a proven history of ministering to others without reproach. It should always be clear who the leader is in each session. Having this clearly established helps both the ministry recipient and the team flow in respect, submission to authority, and order throughout the session. The team leader is the one who leads the recipient in the various prayers within this manual. At any time the leader can allow either the observer or the intercessor to take the lead in praying the prayers; however, the leader is still in charge of the session. After gathering the team members' input, the team leader will be responsible for making decisions concerning when to move forward, what areas need to be addressed, and when the sessions are complete.

Intercessor
The intercessor is present in a deliverance session as someone who is praying for the session to be fruitful.

During the session they are praying for the leader and the recipient, and asking for the breakthrough of deliverance, words of knowledge, or any prophetic revelation the Lord may give. They should pray as the Holy Spirit leads and actively seek prophetic clarity and direction, if necessary. The intercessory role will help in cultivating the presence of God in the session. If at any time the intercessor receives direction from the Lord, they should submit the information in a humble, convenient, and appropriate way to the leader within the session.

Observer

The observer is present in the session to observe the behavior of the recipient. They are looking for signs of deliverance or areas that the team might need to continue praying into. Many times the team leader is distracted by reading and leading the prayers in the manual and needs another person with discernment to help monitor behaviors and signs in the session.

TEAM SELECTION

It is never wise to attempt deeper levels of deliverance alone. Selecting a trustworthy team can be a vital part of a successful deliverance ministry. It is important that the members of your deliverance team understand the calling and assignment you are asking them to participate in. Anyone who wishes to be a part of deliverance ministry needs to be given a full explanation of the expectations that will be upon them when they agree to partner in this type of ministry.

A team member should be living above reproach and understand the requirements of living a holy lifestyle in submission to the will of God. To be a minister in deliverance, I strongly suggest that each person be securely committed to a community of believers with accountability and have a history of faithful devotion to the Lord. Any signs of consistent sinful behavior by any team member must be addressed for the sake of nullifying any attempts of the enemy to bring disruption within the team and its leadership. If any team member is struggling with an ongoing sinful issue, in other words, "practicing" sin, then they should step down from deliverance ministry until restoration and stability have been established.

Team members have the option of whether or not they would like to work with a ministry recipient they already know. If the recipient does not mind, it is fine to do so. The goal is to create as comfortable an atmosphere as possible for all involved. Once a team has been selected, it is recommended they stay together for the duration of the deliverance sessions with a particular recipient. Over time a team learns how to work together in each of their strengths and giftings. While it is not necessary, it can be beneficial for teams that have previously worked together successfully to stay together.

TEAM ETIQUETTE AND PROCEDURE

A team should meet prior to a deliverance session in order to pray and brief. Deliverance sessions should be done in a private, secluded area to ensure confidentiality for the recipient and to avoid unnecessary distraction or disruption. The team leader should have the recipient sign the ministry's Release and Waiver form before beginning the first session. The recipient is also given the handouts *Preparation for Receiving Deliverance* and *Forgiveness* at the start of the first session.

Deliverance sessions should last no longer than two hours. This keeps both team members and the recipient from becoming too fatigued. Completing the sixteen strongholds always takes multiple sessions; the number is determined by the team and can be as few or many as is felt needed. However, ministry should not go on for an extended period of time, such as six months to a year. This will help avoid codependent behavior, a pitfall the team should always be aware of.

All teams members should be friendly and create a comfortable, safe environment in which the recipient can be open and honest. Always get permission from the recipient before touching or placing hands on any area of the body. During the course of the ministry a team should be encouraging, affirming the recipient for their cooperation, always making sure the recipient does not feel embarrassed or ashamed when matters of a private nature come up or if demonic manifestation occurs.

Communication within the team is necessary during the course of a session—it simply needs to be done at an appropriate time, in a non-disruptive way. Whenever a team member receives any type of direction from the Lord concerning the ministry time, they can signal the leader that they feel a sense of direction. The team can decide ahead what way to signal each other.

There will be situations where a person may be taking prescribed medication for their mental, physical, or emotional needs. When an individual is taking prescribed medication it is important to **never** suggest the discontinuation of any medication. The ministry recipient should be advised to consult their doctor. Medical professionals must make that decision.

QUALIFICATIONS FOR THOSE SEEKING DELIVERANCE MINISTRY

Ensuring a person is ready to receive deliverance is one of the most important steps in this type of ministry. A questionnaire (provided in appendix 1) is used to begin the application process. After it has been received, schedule an in-person interview with the ministry director (or a qualified team leader) in order to determine whether the applicant qualifies for this type of personal ministry. During the interview, it is extremely important to make sure those who are seeking ministry are ready and willing to cooperate with the ministry and show a clear determination to make whatever changes are necessary to maintain their freedom. If at any time during the interview you feel the individual is not showing signs of complete willingness and cooperation, then do not continue in the interview process until that cooperation is confirmed or established.

The will and agreement of the individual determines a great deal of their potential to walk out their spiritual freedom once deliverance ministry has begun. Situations may vary depending on the level of spiritual bondage and the individual's ability to coherently communicate. It's crucial to exercise discernment, which can become even clearer with multiple team members' input. Always make sure the recipient's environment and lifestyle is conducive to maintaining deliverance. The questionnaire covers the details necessary to confirm whether the applicant qualifies for this ministry.

In most cases, those seeking deliverance ministry within the church are only at a Level One in terms of demonic influence. They may simply need to apply the basic disciplines of the Christian life, such as daily prayer, reading God's Word, and worship, in order to find freedom. Sometimes it is best to deny applicants Level Two ministry if it is not necessary or not what you feel they need at that time. It is always best to give someone an accurate assessment and to navigate them toward personal responsibility and capability, rather than to potentially create a codependent scenario. Do not allow yourself to be taken advantage of in the name of compassion.

QUESTIONNAIRE AND INTERVIEW

A complete and thorough application process might be the most important part of Level Two deliverance ministry. Gaining as much information as possible and then processing that information with the individual is the most effective way we can determine the negative spiritual influences a person might be under.

Once an applicant has submitted a questionnaire (provided in appendix 1), it should be looked over by the ministry director, followed by an in-person interview. During the interview, the information on the questionnaire should be confirmed and the details surrounding that information be discussed. The person leading the interview should be looking for and highlighting crucial experiences that could help direct the team leader during the actual deliverance sessions. Once the interview is complete and the applicant has been approved to receive deliverance ministry, a team leader should be given the questionnaire, along with the ministry director's assessments and highlights, to review with his or her team. The team should then meet and assess the information, which will give them insight on potential strongholds to target in the person's life. The information in the questionnaire helps identify which strongholds the team is most likely going to encounter. When examining the questionnaire, it is extremely helpful to be as familiar as possible with the sixteen strongholds listed in this manual (chapter 5).

Example scenario: On the questionnaire, a person states they have struggled with nightmares and currently battle anxiety in certain situations. During the interview, it is highlighted that fear is potentially the demonic influence having the most detrimental effect on them. Then the team is given the ministry director's assessments/highlights from the interview, which gives them clarity on which areas need to be addressed in the session. Removing the most obvious influential strongholds first, in this case fear, could make the deliverance sessions more fruitful.

POST-MINISTRY

Discipleship
Once a person has completed all of the Level Two deliverance sessions, it is imperative for him or her to continue in their journey to freedom through ongoing discipleship. Jesus compared the physical body to a house where spirits can reside.

> *"Now when the unclean spirit goes out of a man, it passes through waterless places seeking rest, and does not find it. Then it says, 'I will return to my house from which I came'; and when it comes, it finds it unoccupied, swept, and put in order. Then it goes and takes along with it seven other spirits more wicked than itself, and they go in and live there; and the last state of that man becomes worse than the first."*
> (Matthew 12:43)

Once the house has been cleansed, it is important that the house becomes filled with the Holy Spirit and the truth of the Word of God. A house is filled when a person begins to replace the former thought patterns with the truth of God's Word. They are inviting the Holy Spirit to come and fill them with His presence. Worship, prayer, meditation, and consistent study of God's Word will keep demonic spirits from returning to their once-inhabited home.

The pursuit of discipleship can determine whether a person will maintain their deliverance or not.

The reason many return many times for ministry is the lack of proper discipleship within the Body of Christ. Without it the person becomes dependent on the deliverance ministry, or they lose hope after failing to continue to fight, lacking the proper tools to help. A strong pastoral support structure, accountability, mentorship, or a sense of community can make the difference in a person's ability to maintain the freedom they have just experienced. A helpful post-ministry handout that addresses ongoing discipleship is included in appendix 2 (*Moving Forward after Deliverance*).

A common question is why do we see Jesus casting out demons in such a public way? Was it because He was aware of the people's tendency to fall back into bondage without proper accountability and discipleship? Jesus operated this way mostly due to the culture at that time. Communities were usually small and full of extended family that likely already knew the individual's issues and could help in discipleship/accountability afterward. Also, knowledge of and familiarity with demonic spirits was far more common. It was part of the normal paradigm to attribute various sicknesses and mental issues to demonic influence, making it less shocking and shameful for those being delivered. The context was much different from what we see in the church today, where people could be visiting from another city or be completely unknown in a community and have very little support structure around them.

The goal of deliverance ministry is a person walking out their newfound freedom in Christ, not just the occasional, powerful experience of an evil spirit leaving. This should be the mandate of all deliverance ministries.

Deliverance Procedures: Steps for Personal, Level One, and Level Two Deliverance Sessions

PERSONAL DELIVERANCE: SIX STEPS TO BREAK CYCLES OF DEMONIC INFLUENCE

A person who is in need of deliverance can absolutely find freedom without a ministry team's help. In the Word of God, the Holy Spirit, the blood of Jesus, and the name of Jesus everything has been given in order for a person to receive personal deliverance. It is only when a person is unable to find freedom in this way that deliverance ministry is recommended.

> *His divine power has granted to us everything pertaining to life and godliness, through the true knowledge of Him who called us by His own glory and excellence.*
> (2 Peter 1:3)

> *You are my hiding place; You preserve me from trouble; You surround me with **songs of deliverance**.* (Psalm 32:7)

> *I sought the Lord, and He answered me, and **delivered** me from all my fears.*
> (Psalm 34:4)

Step One: Repent

All involvement with demonic activity must be recognized as sin and repented of. The repentance must be sincere and thorough. It must be in accordance with the truth of God's Word and who He is. Ask the Holy Spirit to show you the areas of sin and lies that the enemy has established in your life. The recognition of our true condition before God will bring forth true repentance and deliverance.

> *If we confess our sins, He is faithful and just to forgive us our sins and to cleanse us from all unrighteousness.* (1 John 1:9 NKJV)

> *Confess your trespasses to one another, and pray for one another, that you may be healed. The effective, fervent prayer of a righteous man avails much.*
> (James 5:16 NKJV)

> *"Repent therefore and be converted, that your sins may be blotted out, so that times of refreshing may come from the presence of the Lord."* (Acts 3:19 NKJV)

> *"Therefore repent of this wickedness of yours, and pray the Lord that, if possible, the intention of your heart may be forgiven you."* (Acts 8:22)

Step Two: Forgive

As we experience different forms of trauma and pain, the enemy will take advantage of our emotional condition and accuse us and everyone else involved. The goal is to get an individual to become angry and bitter at themselves and others. Unforgiveness gives the demon legal right to stay and make its abode with us. Therefore, forgiveness is one of the most important areas to cover when seeking deliverance and freedom from demonic influence. (If needed, refer to the section called *Forgiveness* in chapter 1, and go through the steps listed.)

> *Then Peter came and said to Him, "Lord, how often shall my brother sin against me and I forgive him? Up to seven times?"* (Matthew 18:21)

> *"But if you do not forgive, neither will your Father in heaven forgive your trespasses."* (Mark 11:26 NKJV)

Step Three: Renounce

Along with repentance, we should also declare that we no longer have any agreement with the lies and activity of demons. Renouncing our agreement with darkness and any of its systems and ways will break the stronghold. Renouncing that partnership is powerful and effective when done with an understanding of our true identity in the Spirit.

> *"For assuredly, I say to you, whoever says to this mountain, 'Be removed and be cast into the sea,' and does not doubt in his heart, but believes that those things he says will be done, he will have whatever he says."* (Mark 11:23 NKJV)

Step Four: Command

Take authority over any spirits that have been assigned against you, and command them to leave. Speak with boldness and confidence in who you are as a child of God, and with a heart full of faith, aggressively tell your enemy to go.

> *They were all amazed, so that they debated among themselves, saying, "What is this? A new teaching with authority! He commands even the unclean spirits, and they obey Him."* (Mark 1:27)

Step Five: Receive

We must believe that God has forgiven us and receive both the power and love that is available the moment we turn to Him with sincerity. In some cases, this can be the most difficult part of walking out the breaking of sinful patterns and cycles. After your time of prayer, quiet your mind and, by faith, receive the forgiveness and the cleansing that the Holy Spirit has provided. Meditating on the truth of what the Lord has done will help solidify the work in your life.

"And whatever things you ask in prayer, believing, you will receive."
(Matthew 21:22 NKJV)

"So I say to you, ask, and it will be given to you; seek, and you will find; knock, and it will be opened to you." (Luke 11:9)

But let him ask in faith, with no doubting, for he who doubts is like a wave of the sea driven and tossed by the wind. (James 1:6 NKJV)

You lust and do not have. You murder and covet and cannot obtain. You fight and war. Yet you do not have because you do not ask. (James 4:2 NKJV)

You ask and do not receive, because you ask amiss, that you may spend it on your pleasures. (James 4:3 NKJV)

And whatever we ask we receive from Him, because we keep His commandments and do the things that are pleasing in His sight. (1 John 3:22)

Now this is the confidence that we have in Him, that if we ask anything according to His will, He hears us. And if we know that He hears us, whatever we ask, we know that we have the petitions that we have asked of Him. (1 John 5:14–15 NKJV)

Step Six: Consecrate

It is important to continue to live a life that is consecrated unto the Lord. The enemy will try to return and begin to reconstruct the stronghold that has been torn down. We must be disciplined in our devotion to the Lord in order to continue to move forward in love, freedom, and purity. (See the four areas of consecration listed at the end of this chapter.)

For this is the will of God, your sanctification: that you should abstain from sexual immorality . . . (1 Thessalonians 4:3 NKJV)

Abstain from every form of evil. (1 Thessalonians 5:22)

Beloved, I beg you as sojourners and pilgrims, abstain from fleshly lusts which war against the soul. (1 Peter 2:11 NKJV)

Be angry, and yet do not sin; do not let the sun go down on your anger.
(Ephesians 4:26)

LEVEL ONE DELIVERANCE:
FIVE-STEP PROCEDURE FOR INDIVIDUAL MINISTRY

Level One is the most common form of deliverance needed for born-again believers. One minister rather than an entire team often leads an individual through this level of deliverance. This model can be a useful tool to train for altar ministry.

Step One: Communicate

> *And He was asking him, "What is your name?" And he said to Him, "My name is Legion; for we are many."* (Mark 5:9)

- Step one is to *speak with the person* who you feel may be struggling with demonic oppression.
- *Ask* the individual what is happening and if they feel they need someone to pray with them in agreement for deliverance. They may say, "I am struggling with fear/depression," or "I feel like I have some type of oppression, and God wants to set me free."
- Make sure the person is saved. If so, then *ask if they are aware of any known sin or unforgiveness* in their life.
- You may need to explain how sin and unforgiveness open doors for the enemy to gain access to oppress.
- It is important to emphasize that you are coming alongside the person as they confront the enemy. You are partnering WITH them rather than doing something TO them.

Step Two: Cancel

> *"And his lord, moved with anger, handed him over to the torturers until he should repay all that was owed him."* (Matthew 18:34)

- *Tell the person* you are going to lead them in a prayer of renouncing the evil spirits that are influencing their life. This prayer will include repentance as well as forgiveness.
- *Take authority* over any unclean spirits that may be manifesting during your time of communication and command them to be silent or to cease manifestation. You need the person's complete attention and cooperation.
- *Lead the person in a prayer of repentance, forgiveness* of others, and *renouncement* of all demonic activity or agreement. This prayer is to cancel all legal right for demons to remain.
- Never assume the person has been completely honest about issues of sin or unforgiveness. Be prepared for more issues to arise. If more issues do arise, the minister should *lead the individual through the repent/forgive/renounce prayer for the new issue.*

Step Three: Cleanse

> *... so that He might sanctify her, having cleansed her by the washing of water with the word.* (Ephesians 5:26)

- At this point it is appropriate to *minister inner healing* to any area that has been brought up. The issues of pain don't have to be completely resolved (since that is usually a process), but each area

should be surrendered to Jesus. Pray for the person to receive healing from the effects of sins committed against them, to receive God's forgiveness, and to receive healing from the effects of the sins they have committed themselves.
- Take a moment to *speak God's truths* over the individual in any area where they have believed the lies of the enemy.
- Take time to *ask the Holy Spirit to come* with His presence and to direct the person's heart into the love of God. This is a helpful way to remove the ground that the enemy has used as a stronghold of oppression and to equip the person in the knowledge of God.
- *Encourage the individual to receive* and meditate on the truth that has been spoken over them and the love that God has shown to them.

Step Four: Command

> *They were all amazed, so that they debated among themselves, saying, "What is this? A new teaching with authority! He commands even the unclean spirits, and they obey Him." (Mark 1:27)*

- Now that the individual has prayed a prayer of renouncing the spirits and receiving healing, forgiveness, and truth, *enter into a time of warfare prayer* in agreement with them.
  - Again, emphasize that you are coming alongside the person as they confront the enemy—partnering WITH them, not doing something TO them.
  - Be sure that the individual is in cooperation and is engaging along with your prayers.
- *Pray with faith and authority* for demons to leave.
  - Do not mention the name of any spirits unless the person has already mentioned them. We do not want people to think they have more spirits in or around them than they actually have.
  - There is no need to shout at this point or to do any dramatic movements of any kind. Demons respond to the authority of Jesus, not to volume or display of dramatic tactics.
  - If you were given any specific information concerning a demonic spirit being present, speak directly to that spirit (fear, infirmity, etc.). For example, "In the name of Jesus, we command every unclean spirit to go right now. Fear, go. Infirmity, go. Leave in Jesus' name!"
  - There may be some manifestations as the spirits leave (e.g. coughing, sneezing, burping, vomiting, yawning, etc.). However, a person does not need to manifest in order for deliverance to be achieved or proven.
- If a person begins to manifest a demon to the point where he or she loses consciousness, command the spirit to submit to the authority of Jesus. Do not continue the deliverance at that time. The situation has now elevated to a Level Two in deliverance, and, for the sake of time and thoroughness, the person will need to be referred to a more in-depth deliverance ministry.

Step Five: Consecrate

> *"When the unclean spirit goes out of a man, it passes through waterless places seeking rest, and not finding any, it says, 'I will return to my house from which I came.' And when it comes, it finds it swept and put in order. Then it goes and takes along seven other spirits more evil than itself, and they go in and live there; and the last state of that man becomes worse than the first." (Luke 11:24–26)*

> *Afterward Jesus found him in the temple and said to him, "Behold, you have become well; do not sin anymore, so that nothing worse happens to you."* (John 5:14)

- If you and the individual feel that the oppression has lifted, continue by praying and prophesying over him or her. If not, continue to pray for the situation as time allows.
- Declare over them their freedom in Christ.
- End your time of ministry with the individual by blessing them with the fullness of the Holy Spirit.
- Be sure to encourage the person to live a consecrated life in order to maintain freedom.

LEVEL TWO DELIVERANCE: TEN-STEP PROCEDURE FOR TEAM MINISTRY*

* The prayers used in this procedure can be found in order in chapters 4 and 5. Each team member should have a copy of the ministry manual, but the ministry recipient does not. They will be verbally led in prayer by the team leader, leaving them free to keep their spirit open and undistracted.

Step One: Deliverance Team Briefing
- A team leader will be appointed by the ministry's director and its leadership based on schedule and availability, and they will select their team members. A director could suggest team members whose giftings may be needed. The ministry recipient's information and ministry director's interview assessments are passed to the team leader, who will contact the recipient to set up the session dates and times.
- The team leader will brief the team concerning the recipient sometime prior to the first session (obvious strongholds were assessed through the interview process). A team briefing is suggested before each session.
- Go into a time of prayer as a team. Pray over each other, over the room, for the recipient, and for protection over the team's family members and loved ones.

Step Two: Greeting the Recipient of Ministry
- The team leader will invite the person in and introduce all of the team members. Be sure to smile and be as friendly as possible—create an environment of no intimidation for the recipient.
- The team leader will go over the procedure, explaining everything to the recipient.
  - Explain what prayers will be prayed and how the recipient will be participating.
  - Explain where the team will be placing their hands, and get permission for that.
  - Ask if they have any questions or concerns.
  - Highly emphasize the necessity of their involvement and cooperation during the deliverance session.
- The leader will explain that the team will be addressing the realm of the demonic and not the recipient personally. This is very important, so that we're not creating insecurity in an individual. It is our goal to treat the person with as much dignity as possible.

Step Three: Lead the Recipient in the Prayer of Submission to the Lordship of Jesus Christ
- The team leader will lead the recipient in the initial prayer of *repentance, forgiveness of others, and submission to the lordship of Jesus Christ*. This prayer is found in chapter 4.

- Emphasize the importance of forgiveness, and show the recipient where in the prayer it has been designated for them to state any people they need to forgive.
- The other members of the team both observe and intercede during the prayer.

Step Four: Communion (Optional)
- Communion will be led by the team leader; all members of the team will partake of it.
- The prayer will be one of remembrance and thankfulness to God for the body and the blood of Jesus.
- The team must stay in a mode of discerning and intercession for the recipient during holy communion.

Step Five: Break the Power of Any Soul Ties
We must understand that a soul tie occurs when two people are involved in sexual misconduct together. As a result of the sexual union, according to Matthew 19:5–6, the two have been joined together. This connection can cause a person to be negatively affected both spiritually and emotionally unless they consciously break with the union.
- Follow the *Prayer to Break Soul Ties* in chapter 4.
- Start by asking the recipient to pray a prayer of repentance to the Lord for their sexual misconduct with everyone to whom it may apply (assure confidentiality).
- The team then prays, asking that the recipient's spirit be loosed from each individual, in the name of Jesus, according to Matthew 18:18–19.
- Ask the individual to tell their spirit to forget the union, and to tell their mind, will, and emotions to release any responsibility for the others involved, in Jesus' name.
- Ask the Lord to heal any wounds and to remove all negative memories, in Jesus' name.

Step Six: Break the Power of Generational Demonic Curses
- Follow the *Prayer to Break Generational Assignments and Demonic Curses* in chapter 4.
- The effects of a curse can mostly be attributed to a familiar spirit. As you break the curses, be sure to address any manifestations that may be occurring due to a familiar spirit.
- All the members of the team focus directly and agree in the prayer led by the team leader.

Step Seven (as needed): Break the Power of Freemasonry and Witchcraft
- It is important to make sure that the individual and/or their immediate family members have had clear and obvious involvement in the area of both Freemasonry and witchcraft before incorporating this step. If this step is needed because of involvement with:
  - Witchcraft: follow the *Prayer to Break the Power of Witchcraft* in chapter 4.
  - Freemasonry: follow the *Prayer for Release from Freemasonry* and *Prayer to Break the Power of Witchcraft* in appendix 3.

Step Eight: Begin the Renouncement of the 16 Strongholds
- Follow the *Prayer to Break Strongholds* in chapter 4. Specifics for each of the sixteen strongholds and their manifestations are listed in chapter 5. Plug these into the outlined prayer. Each team member should have a copy of the ministry manual to follow.
- Begin with any strongholds identified by the interview, ministry director, or team as causing the individual the most trouble.

- The team leader will lead the recipient through renouncing each manifestation listed underneath the stronghold being addressed. The other team members will stay in an attitude of warfare, intercession, and discernment.
- After all manifestations are renounced, the team leader will pray to break the stronghold.

  Example of Breaking the Stronghold prayer:
  "We command any spirit associated with the stronghold of Antichrist to leave according to the Word of God, in Jesus' name. We take authority over you and cast you out in the mighty name of Jesus. All your works are hereby canceled and you will not have control of this person any longer."
- Continue to address the stronghold until all physical manifestations are gone or until the team and the recipient feel a release to move on.
- Move on to the next stronghold, and continue this process until all sixteen have been covered. It may be necessary to go on and break another stronghold before the power of a certain one will be broken. Discernment and communication amongst the team is critical during this process. Communication must be done in an orderly way and with respect toward the team leader.
- If at any time the leader becomes tired, he or she can pass the leadership to another, in order to continue the ministry.
- No session should last longer than two hours. If a session is not completed but needs to end, seal up your time of ministry with the Holy Spirit and schedule a time to reconvene.

Step Nine: Blessing, Encouragement, and Prophecy
- At the end of the deliverance session the team will bless the recipient and speak words of encouragement and life. Follow the *Prayer of Blessing* in chapter 4.
- Pray that the Holy Spirit would seal the ministry and protect the person as they go in the will of God. Feel free to give any prophetic words that the Lord may have given you during the session.
- Be sure to affirm the recipient and build them up in faith.
- This blessing, encouragement, and prophecy should be done at the end of each session.
- Outline for the ministry recipient the importance of maintaining their freedom through consecration and ongoing discipleship.
- After their final session, provide them with a copy of the post-ministry handout *Moving Forward after Deliverance* and the *Deliverance Ministry Feedback* form (located in the appendices), which they can fill out and return at their convenience.

Step Ten: Submit Deliverance Session Report
- The team leader should fill out the *Deliverance Session Report* (located in appendix 1), getting input from the team members, and submit it to the ministry director.

MAINTAINING FREEDOM

After a person finds freedom through any type of deliverance ministry it is crucial to maintain that freedom by separating themselves from any way that the enemy would seek to return. By living a life of consecration (focused devotion), we can greatly reduce the enemy's ability to manipulate or deceive. There are four primary areas where someone can consecrate their life to both maintain their newfound freedom and block any further deception from the enemy.

Four Areas of Consecration

1. Time

> *How long will you slumber, O sluggard? When will you rise from your sleep?*
> (Proverbs 6:9 NKJV)

> *So teach us to number our days, that we may gain a heart of wisdom.*
> (Psalm 90:12 NKJV)

2. Money

> *"For where your treasure is, there your heart will be also."* (Luke 12:34)

> *For the love of money is a root of all kinds of evil, for which some have strayed from the faith in their greediness, and pierced themselves through with many sorrows.*
> (1 Timothy 6:10 NKJV)

3. Mouth

> *And the tongue is a fire, a world of iniquity. The tongue is so set among our members that it defiles the whole body, and sets on fire the course of nature; and it is set on fire by hell.* (James 3:6 NKJV)

4. Eyes

> *I will set nothing wicked before my eyes.* (Psalm 101:3 NKJV)

> *I have made a covenant with my eyes; why then should I look upon a young woman?*
> (Job 31:1 NKJV)

It is important to note and understand that God has given the human race the power of free will. This gives everyone the ability to either agree or disagree with both truth and lies. Demons can only have power over us to the extent that we are in agreement with them.

Ongoing Discipleship

Understand that the enemy will try to return, but Christians have been given everything they need to maintain their freedom without fear. A life of ongoing discipleship is essential. The following points are included in the post-ministry handout the recipient will receive.

- Daily worship, prayer, meditation on God's Word, and consistent study of God's Word will keep demonic spirits from taking back the ground they have lost.
- Have faith in what the Lord has done and the truth of His love for you.
- Be confident in the truth of your identity and authority in Jesus Christ.
- Stay connected with or get involved in your local church fellowship. Accountability and ongoing discipleship is crucial to your growth and freedom.
- Try to find other strong believers in Jesus Christ and develop godly friendships. Avoid going back to relationships you know aren't right for you.
- Keep closed all previously open doors to the enemy that might have been revealed in your time of ministry (music, movies, relationships, etc. that you know had negative influences over your life).
- Understand that total deliverance can be a process, and ongoing counseling, emotional healing, and the restoration of your thought patterns can take time. Be patient. Stay faithful.

4

SPIRITUAL DELIVERANCE PRAYERS

The following prayers are listed in the order in which they are used during the Level Two deliverance procedure outlined in the previous chapter. The team leader leads the recipient in these prayers. During portions labeled "team leader," the team members are agreeing, but the leader is the only one verbally praying.

PRAYER OF SUBMISSION TO THE LORDSHIP OF JESUS CHRIST [1]

(Led by the team leader, repeated by the recipient.)

"Dear Lord Jesus, I believe that You are the Son of God, that You died on the cross for my sins, and that You rose again from the dead. I confess You as my Lord and Savior; I repent of all my sins. I repent for and renounce all demonic spirits that I have allowed to enter my life."

"Lord, I forgive all those who have wronged me or harmed me. I lay down all resentment, all hatred, and all rebellion. In particular, I forgive _____ *(insert names)*. Lord, I ask You to forgive me and cleanse me by Your precious blood. Right now I accept Your love and forgiveness into my life." *(Look them in the eye and tell them they are forgiven.)*

"I take authority over every demonic spirit influencing my life and I command them to leave me in the name of Jesus. Amen."

PRAYER TO BREAK SOUL TIES

Recipient:

"Lord Jesus, I repent for any and all ungodly relationships. I repent for opening my life up physically, spiritually, and emotionally to a union that was not a part of Your plan for my life. I repent for all sexual misconduct, emotional dependency, and spiritual influence that might have occurred during these relationships. Lord, I release all persons, places, or things that the enemy has used to try to control my life."

Team leader:
> "I now command that your spirit be loosed from each and every individual, location, and object in the name of Jesus. We declare that any ungodly union be broken and cut off from your soul and spirit, in Jesus' name."

Recipient:
> "I command my spirit to forget the ungodly unions and memories, and command my mind, will, and emotions to release any responsibility for the others involved, in Jesus' name."

Team leader:
> "Lord, I ask that You release healing to any and every wound _____ (recipient's name) may have received through these associations. I ask that You cleanse and restore her/his heart to complete wholeness, in Jesus' name."

PRAYER TO BREAK GENERATIONAL ASSIGNMENTS AND DEMONIC CURSES

With the full agreement and cooperation of the individual, go into a time of prayer, commanding that, in the name of Jesus, all generational demonic curses be broken. The team declares to the demonic realm that these curses and assignments will not continue into further generations.

> "We cancel and break the power of all curses that have been allowed through the generations by way of familiar spirits—we cancel your assignment and command you to leave, in the name of Jesus. Every curse or spell that has been projected by the occult is now broken by the blood of Jesus. We declare the curses will no longer be allowed to rest upon any future generations of this household and family."

Ask God to restore all that has been stolen, and reclaim all the blessings of a child of God.

In some cases involving the occult or false religion, there can be many vows or curses that are spoken over a person's life and family as they are initiated into the organization. Those vows or curses must sometimes be specifically mentioned and broken by those who have been involved or affected. Freemasonry initiation rites are an example of vows that need to be specifically addressed for the demonic curse to be broken in cases of high-level covenants and blood rituals. If needed, a prayer to break witchcraft follows, and an extensive prayer breaking Freemasonry is included in appendix 3 (this may require a separate deliverance session).

PRAYER TO BREAK THE POWER OF WITCHCRAFT [2]

(Use if applicable. Prayer is led by the team leader, repeated by the recipient.)

These prayers are to be prayed with those who have clearly exhibited the effects of high-level participation or familiar association with the occult or satanic ritual abuse. Do not use these prayers unless it has been determined to be necessary by the team leader.

"Heavenly Father, I love You, and I will serve You and You alone. I declare that Satan's control in my life is over, and his assignments are broken, in Jesus' name."

"I repent of and renounce all contact with witchcraft and the occult, willingly or in ignorance, known or unknown."

"I repent of and renounce all contact with witchcraft and the occult by my ancestors."

"I repent of, renounce, and break all power that I have received from any and all involvement with witchcraft and the occult. I break all agreements, all pacts, all contracts, and all deals made with Satan!"

"In Jesus' mighty name and by the power of His shed blood, I repent of and renounce all involvement with Ouija boards, Magic 8-Balls, séances, astrology, horoscopes, fortune telling, and ESP. I repent of and renounce all involvement with palm readers, tarot cards, psychic readings, the third eye, levitation, and communication with the dead, as well as all forms of deception, control, manipulation, and rebellion."

"I repent of and renounce all involvement with black magic, white magic, yoga, meditations, crystals, fetishes, and automatic handwriting."

"I break all chants, spells, vows, covenants, and incantations, including the effects of all Freemasonry."

"I renounce all sacrifices, including blood sacrifices, both animal or human."

"I break all blood oaths and blood vows."

PRAYER TO BREAK STRONGHOLDS

The sixteen strongholds listed in the following chapter have been gathered from the testimony of Scripture and are a useful prayer guide when addressing spiritual influences. They are not to be referenced as demons themselves but are the results of demonic activity. The strongholds and all their manifestations are to be renounced, and any sinful agreements are to be repented of. The deliverance team should begin with any stronghold specifically identified as influential in the ministry recipient's life and then continue until all sixteen strongholds have been broken.

During this prayer, the ministry recipient will repent from and renounce agreement with the specific stronghold, and then the team leader will lead them through renunciation of each listed manifestation. Once done, the leader and team members will command the specific spirit to leave and the spiritual stronghold to be broken. Finally, the leader should bless the recipient with the associated blessing (included at the end of each stronghold listed).

In case of a demonic manifestation, continue commanding the spirit to leave until deliverance is achieved. It might be necessary to repeat the renouncing and repentance prayers in order for the demonic spirit's hold to be broken.

Example Prayer (apply to each stronghold):
Recipient:
"I repent from and renounce any sinful behavior or agreement with the stronghold of _____ (*for instance,* Antichrist) in the name of Jesus Christ."

Team leader:
Lead the recipient through renouncing and repenting of all the manifestations or fruit listed under the stronghold being addressed.

SPIRITUAL DELIVERANCE PRAYERS | 33

Team leader:

Once all the renouncing and repentance prayers have been prayed, begin to command all spirits associated with the stronghold of _____ (*for instance,* Antichrist) to leave:

"We command every unclean spirit to go, in Jesus' name. Your deception is broken, your power is broken, and you must leave now, in Jesus' name."

Continue in this vein of prayer until all the team members and the ministry recipient feel the release to move on to the next stronghold.

PRAYER OF BLESSING [3]

(To be prayed over the recipient at the conclusion of each deliverance session.)

"In the name of Jesus Christ, I bless you *(recipient's name)* with the promises of God, which are yes and amen. I pray the Holy Spirit will make you healthy and strong in body, mind, and spirit to move in faith and expectancy. May God's angels be with you to protect and keep you."

- God bless you with the love of the Father, that you may know His love.
- God bless you with ability, with abundance, and with an assurance of His love and grace.
- God bless you with clear direction, with a controlled and disciplined life.
- God bless you with courage and creativity.
- God bless you with spiritual perception of His truth.
- God bless you with great faith, and with His favor and with man's.
- God bless you with good health and a good marriage *(if applicable—i.e., recipient is not called to celibacy).*
- God bless your hands to bless others.
- God bless you with happiness, fulfillment, contentment, hope, and a good outlook on life.
- God bless you with a listening ear and with a long life and an obedient heart to the Spirit of God.
- God bless you with His peace, with pleasant speech, a pleasant personality, with promotion, protection, provision, safety, and strength.
- God bless you with success, trust, and wisdom.

"God bless you with goodness and mercy following you all the days of your life, and may you dwell in the house of the Lord forever. The Lord bless you and keep you. The Lord make His face to shine upon you and give you peace, the peace of God that surpasses all understanding. I bless you, *(recipient's name)*, in the name of Jesus Christ. Amen."

Notes

[1] Based on "Deliverance Prayer," Teresa Castleman and John A. Kilpatrick, *The Deliverance Manual* (Pensacola: Brownsville Assembly of God, 1996-97), 22. Used by permission.

[2] Reprinted from *Deliverance Training Manual*, William Sudduth and Judith Sudduth (Stephens City, VA: RAM Inc., 2000). Used by permission.

[3] Based on "Blessing," Teresa Castleman and John A. Kilpatrick, *The Deliverance Manual* (Pensacola: Brownsville Assembly of God, 1996-97), 52–53. Used by permission.

THE SIXTEEN STRONGHOLDS

The sixteen strongholds[1] in this chapter have been gathered from the testimony of Scripture. Using the *Prayer to Break Strongholds* in the previous chapter, a ministry team and ministry recipient should pray through each one of the following sixteen strongholds. Once a stronghold and all its listed manifestations have been repented of and renounced, all spirits associated with it can be commanded to leave and the stronghold broken. A blessing (included) is then prayed over the ministry recipient.

STRONGHOLD OF ANTICHRIST

Every spirit that does not confess that Jesus Christ has come in the flesh is not of God. And this is the spirit of the Antichrist... (1 John 4:3 NKJV)

Antichrist: anything that denies or opposes Christ.

Prayer:

I renounce the Stronghold of Antichrist, every spirit of Antichrist, and its manifestations and fruit.

I repent of and renounce (any spirit that):
- Denies the deity of Christ
- Denies the Atonement (Atonement: the reconciliation of God and humankind through Jesus Christ[2])
- Comes against Christ and His teaching
- Suppresses ministries
- Secular humanism
- A Jezebel spirit
- Operating in division and control
- Worldly speech and actions
- Profanity
- Lawlessness (Lawlessness: rebellion against God, whether viewed as the condition of one's life or as specific actions that demonstrate a determined refusal to acknowledge God[3])
- The Accuser and the Deceiver
- Any serpent spirits
- A dragon spirit
- Any ungodly music
- Legalism, ritualism, or formalism
- All false doctrines within:
  - Mormonism
  - Pharisaism
  - Nazism
  - Buddhism
  - New Age
  - Catholicism
  - Unitarianism
  - Communism
  - Hinduism
  - Jehovah's Witnesses

Break the Stronghold of Antichrist and command all spirits to leave.
Bless them with the Spirit of truth.

We are from God; he who knows God listens to us; he who is not from God does not listen to us. By this we know the spirit of truth and the spirit of error. (1 John 4:6)

STRONGHOLD OF BONDAGE

For you did not receive the spirit of bondage again to fear, but you received the Spirit of adoption by whom we cry out, "Abba, Father." (Romans 8:15 NKJV)

Bondage: a state of being bound usually by compulsion, servitude, or subject to a controlling person or force.[4]

Prayer:

I renounce the Stronghold of Bondage and its manifestations and fruit.

I repent of and renounce:
- Bondage to fear
- Bondage to all addictions:
  - Drugs
  - Cigarettes
  - Sex
  - Computers
  - Alcohol
  - Food
  - TV
  - Shopping, etc.
- Bondage to lust
- A bound spirit
- Mind-binding spirit
- Bondage to sin
- Compulsive behavior
- Compulsive sin
- Captivity to Satan
- Servant to corruption
- Religious bondage
- Idolatry
- Bondage to ambition and achievement
- Bondage to bitterness
- Bondage to oppression
- Spiritual blindness
- Fear of death
- Spiritual death
- Control
- Familiar spirit of bondage

Break the Stronghold of Bondage and command all spirits to leave.
Bless them with the Spirit of adoption and liberty.

For you did not receive the spirit of bondage again to fear, but you received the Spirit of adoption by whom we cry out, "Abba, Father." (Romans 8:15 NKJV)

STRONGHOLD OF A DEAF AND DUMB SPIRIT

He rebuked the unclean spirit, saying to it, "Deaf and dumb spirit, I command you, come out of him and enter him no more!" (Mark 9:25 NKJV)

Deaf and dumb: the inability to hear or speak, both naturally and spiritually.

Prayer:

I renounce the Deaf and Dumb spirit and its manifestations and fruit.

I repent of and renounce:

- Dumbness and muteness, including spiritual
- Deafness (spiritual deafness)
- Blindness (spiritual blindness)
- Drowning
- Compulsive behavior
- Mental illness
- Madness
- Insanity
- Retardation
- Senility
- Schizophrenia
- Paranoia
- Hearing voices
- Hallucinations
- Palsy
- Attention-deficit disorder (ADD) and Attention-deficit/hyperactivity disorder (ADHD)
- Dissociative identity disorder (MPD)
- Crippling
- Crying and frequent tears
- Ear problems
- Foaming at the mouth
- Alzheimer's
- Gnashing of teeth (teeth grinding)
- Pining away
- Prostration
- Burning myself
- Suicide (attempts and suicidal thinking)
- Chemical imbalance (bipolar)
- Seizures and epilepsy
- Self-hatred
- Self-mutilation
- Eating disorders
- A familiar spirit of deaf and dumb

Break the Stronghold of a Deaf and Dumb Spirit and command all spirits to leave.
Bless them with resurrection life and gifts of healing.

> *But if the Spirit of Him who raised Jesus from the dead dwells in you, He who raised Christ Jesus from the dead will also give life to your mortal bodies through His Spirit who dwells in you.* (Romans 8:11)

> *. . . to another faith by the same Spirit, and to another gifts of healing by the one Spirit . . .* (1 Corinthians 12:9)

STRONGHOLD OF DEATH

The last enemy that will be destroyed is death. (1 Corinthians 15:26 NKJV)

Death: the action or fact of dying or being killed; the end of the life of a person (spiritually, emotionally, and/or physically).[2]

Prayer:

I renounce the spirit of death and the curse of premature death.

I break all plans of the enemy, and I break every assignment against my life due to:
- Accidents
- Assault
- Abduction
- Injury
- Illness
- Random acts of violence
- Disease
- Cancer
- Suicide

I break every assignment of:
- Abortion
- Miscarriages
- Death
- Destruction
- Familiar spirit of death

I break every assignment of death to my:
- Ministry
- Anointing
- Relationships
- Marriage
- Emotions
- Finances

Break the Stronghold of Death and command all spirits to leave.
Bless them with life.

> *"I call heaven and earth to witness against you today, that I have set before you life and death, the blessing and the curse. So choose life in order that you may live, you and your descendants."* (Deuteronomy 30:19)

STRONGHOLD OF DIVINATION

Now it happened, as we went to prayer, that a certain slave girl possessed with a spirit of divination met us, who brought her masters much profit by fortune-telling.
(Acts 16:16 NKJV)

Divination: the art or practice that seeks to foresee or foretell future events or discover hidden knowledge usually by the interpretation of omens or by the aid of demonic powers.[4]

Prayer:
I renounce the Stronghold of Divination and Witchcraft and its manifestations and fruit.

I repent of and renounce:
- Lust for power and control
- Involvement with:
    - Fortune-tellers, soothsayers, and psychics
    - Stargazers, zodiac, and horoscopes
    - False prophets
    - Warlocks, witches, sorcerers, and wizards
    - Hypnotists and enchanters
- All spirit guides (Spirit guide: a disembodied spirit used to give direction or protection, often referenced by psychics, mediums, and spiritists)
- All animal guides (Animal guide: a spirit guide, associated with Native American cultures, that gives insight)
- All indigenous witchcraft
- Astral projection (Astral projection: a term used to describe when the human spirit leaves the body and travels separately from the physical body)
- Druidic and Celtic witchcraft
- Occultism
- Rebellion
- Drug abuse
- Birth charts
- All magic, black or white
- A serpent spirit
- Spiritism (Spiritism: the belief that the dead communicate with the living)
- A Jezebel spirit (divisive, controlling, and seducing)
- Water witching
  (Water witching: locating water sources by way of divination)
- Divination
- Selfishness
- Mind control
  (Mind control: purposely able to go in and out of consciousness)
- Manipulation

- Automatic handwriting, and handwriting analysis (Automatic handwriting: writing produced by the subconscious due to demonic influence)
- Wicca (Wicca: religious cult of modern witchcraft)
- Familiar spirit of divination and witchcraft

Break the Stronghold of Divination and command all spirits to leave.
Bless them with the Holy Spirit and gifts.

> *...to another faith by the same Spirit, and to another gifts of healing by the one Spirit, and to another the effecting of miracles, and to another prophecy, and to another the distinguishing of spirits, to another various kinds of tongues, and to another the interpretation of tongues. But one and the same Spirit works all these things, distributing to each one individually just as He wills. For even as the body is one and yet has many members, and all the members of the body, though they are many, are one body, so also is Christ.* (1 Corinthians 12:9–12)

STRONGHOLD OF ERROR

We are of God. He who knows God hears us; he who is not of God does not hear us. By this we know the spirit of truth and the spirit of error. (1 John 4:6 NKJV)

Error: the opposite of truth; wrong in conduct or judgment.[2] That which is false or twisted.

Prayer:

I renounce the Stronghold of Error and its manifestations and fruit.

I repent of and renounce:

- A spirit of error
- All false prophecies spoken over me by anyone, including myself
- Unsubmissiveness
- Hyper-spirituality
- All false doctrines within:
    - Mormonism
    - Pharisaism
    - Buddhism
    - Hinduism
    - New Age movement
    - Unitarianism
    - Communism
    - Nazism
    - Jehovah's Witnesses
- Scripture manipulation
- An unteachable spirit
- Mixing the holy with the profane
- A defensive and argumentative spirit
- Sympathy for the devil
- Contentiousness
- Servant of corruption
- Having a form of godliness but denying its power
- Mental confusion and fears
- Physical illness and pain
- Depression
- Dullness of comprehension
- Spiritual hindrances to:
    - Prayer
    - Bible study
    - Listening to sermons
    - Moving in the gifts of the Spirit
- Faith principles that have come in through error
- Familiar spirit of error

Break the Stronghold of Error and command all spirits to leave.
Bless them with the Spirit of truth.

> *We are from God; he who knows God listens to us; he who is not from God does not listen to us. By this we know the spirit of truth and the spirit of error.* (1 John 4:6)

> *Create in me a clean heart, O God, and renew a steadfast spirit within me.* (Psalm 51:10)

STRONGHOLD OF FEAR

For God has not given us a spirit of fear, but of power and of love and of a sound mind. (2 Timothy 1:7 NKJV)

Fear: an unpleasant emotion caused by the belief that someone or something is dangerous, likely to cause pain, or a threat.[2]

Prayer:

I renounce the Stronghold of Fear and its manifestations and fruit.

I repent of and renounce:

- A spirit of fear
- A critical spirit
- Not trusting
- Doubt
- Worry
- Unbelief
- Anxiety
- Stress
- Panic attacks
- Migraines
- Torment
- Horror
- Terror
- Nightmares
- Fear of the dark
- Fear of death
    - Death of self
    - Death of family
- Being reclusive and hermit-like
- Excessive introversion
- Feeling alone
- Fear of man
- Fear of relationships
- Fear of molestation or rape
- Fear of rejection
- Fear of abandonment
- Excessive extroversion
- Heart attacks
- Fear of authority
- Fear of saying no
- Fear of failure
- Perfectionism
- Not being good enough
- Fear of food
- Unhealthy fear of God
- All phobias
    - Heights
    - Animals
    - Spiders
    - Water, etc.
- Fear that came in from horror movies
- Familiar spirit of fear

Break the Stronghold of Fear and command all spirits to leave.
Bless them with love, power, and a sound mind.

For God has not given us a spirit of fear, but of power and of love and of a sound mind. (2 Timothy 1:7 NKJV)

STRONGHOLD OF HARLOTRY

"They do not direct their deeds toward turning to their God, for the spirit of harlotry is in their midst, and they do not know the Lord." (Hosea 5:4 NKJV)

Harlotry: a form of prostitution, adultery, and lewdness.

Prayer:

I renounce the Stronghold of Harlotry (Prostitution and Whoredoms) and its manifestations and fruit.

I repent of and renounce:
- All unfaithfulness
- Adultery
- Fornication
- Prostitution (spirit, soul, and body)
- Love of money
- Materialism
- Love of control
- Love of power
- Excessive appetites
- Worldliness
- Worldly speech and actions
- Idolatry
- Chronic dissatisfaction
- Love of self
- Self-reward
- Familiar spirit of whoredoms

Break the Stronghold of Harlotry and command all spirits to leave.
Bless them with the Spirit of God and a pure spirit.

> *That He would grant you, according to the riches of His glory, to be strengthened with power through His Spirit in the inner man.* (Ephesians 3:16)

STRONGHOLD OF HAUGHTINESS

Pride goes before destruction, and a haughty spirit before a fall.
(Proverbs 16:18 NKJV)

Haughtiness: the appearance or quality of being arrogantly superior and disdainful.[2]

Prayer:
I renounce the Stronghold of Haughtiness and its manifestations and fruit.

I repent of and renounce:

- Arrogance
- Vanity
- Pride
- Rationalization in the area of pride
- Professional pride
- National pride
- Regional pride
- Bragging and boastfulness
- Egotism
- Scornfulness
- Obstinance (Obstinate: stubbornly refusing to change one's opinion or chosen course of action, despite attempts to persuade one to do so[2])
- Self-righteousness
- Dictatorship and control
- Overbearingness and domineering (Domineer: assert one's will over another in an arrogant way[2])
- Manipulation and control
- Rejection of God and rejection of authority
- Rebellion
- Better-than-others attitude
- Exalted feelings
- Gossip
- Division
- Dissention (Dissension: disagreement that leads to discord[2])
- Contentiousness (Contentious: a person who likes to argue or quarrel)
- Strife
- Self-deception
- Idleness
- Performance
- Attention seeking and being demonstrative
- Interruption
- Impatience
- Always being right
- Criticism and faultfinding
- Haughtiness that came in through abuse and hurt
- A familiar spirit of haughtiness

Break the Stronghold of Haughtiness and command all spirits to leave.
Bless them with a humble and contrite spirit.

> *It is better to be humble in spirit with the lowly than to divide the spoil with the proud.* (Proverbs 16:19)

STRONGHOLD OF HEAVINESS

To give them . . . the garment of praise for the spirit of heaviness. (Isaiah 61:3 NKJV)

Heaviness: the state or quality of being heavy, causing weariness, restlessness, or lack of interest.

Prayer:
I renounce the Stronghold of Heaviness and its manifestations and fruit.

I repent of and renounce:
- Excessive sorrow and grief
- Self-pity
- A broken heart
- Inner hurts
- False responsibility
- Suicidal thoughts
- Gluttony
- Loneliness
- Heaviness and depression
- Excessive mourning
- Discouragement and despair
- Dejection and hopelessness
- Rejection, insecurity, and abandonment
- Inferiority and low self-esteem
- Results of sexual abuse
- Lack of praise and un-pacified emotions
- Suppressed emotions: fear, anger, rage, violence, and hatred
- Self-hate
- Self-mutilation
- Insomnia
- Chemical imbalance
- Familiar spirit of heaviness

Break the Stronghold of Heaviness and command all spirits to leave.
Bless them with the Comforter, the garment of praise, and the oil of joy.

> *"When the Helper [Comforter] comes, whom I will send to you from the Father, that is the Spirit of truth who proceeds from the Father, He will testify about Me."* John 15:26)

> *To grant those who mourn in Zion, giving them a garland instead of ashes, the oil of gladness instead of mourning, the mantle of praise instead of a spirit of fainting. So they will be called oaks of righteousness, the planting of the LORD, that He may be glorified.* (Isaiah 61:3)

STRONGHOLD OF INFIRMITY

And behold, there was a woman who had a spirit of infirmity eighteen years, and was bent over and could in no way raise herself up. (Luke 13:11 NKJV)

Infirmity: a physical or mental weakness, illness, ailment, disease, disorder, sickness, or affliction.

Prayer:

I renounce the Stronghold of Infirmity and its manifestations and fruit; and I break every assignment of infirmity past, present, and future.

I repent of allowing and agreeing with the assignment of, and I renounce:
- Hypochondria
- A bent body and spine (i.e., scoliosis)
- Chemical imbalance
- High fever
- All mental illness
- Bipolar disorder
- Impotence (frail and lame)
- Arthritis and a root of bitterness
- Diabetes
- All oppression
- Pain and affliction
- All lingering disorders
- TB and emphysema
- Cancer
- Tumors and cysts
- Weakness (tiredness and fatigue)
- All infections (viral, bacterial, and fungal)
- Asthma (allergies and hay fever)
- Epilepsy and seizures
- Fear of infirmity, sickness, and disease
- Familiar spirit of infirmity, sickness, and disease

Break the Stronghold of Infirmity and command all spirits to leave.
Bless them with the Spirit of life and gifts of healing.

> *For the law of the Spirit of life in Christ Jesus has set you free from the law of sin and of death.* (Romans 8:2)

> *. . . to another faith by the same Spirit, and to another gifts of healing by the one Spirit.* (1 Corinthians 12:9)

STRONGHOLD OF JEALOUSY

"And if feelings [a spirit] of jealousy come over her husband and he suspects his wife and she is impure—or if he is jealous and suspects her even though she is not impure—" (Numbers 5:14 NIV)

Jealousy: an emotion of envy of someone or their achievements and advantages.[2]

Prayer:

I renounce the Stronghold of Jealousy and its manifestations and fruit.

I repent of and renounce:
- Jealousy
- Murder
- Revenge and spite
- Cruelty
- Extreme competition
- Causing divisions
- Coveting
- Selfishness
- Envy
- Strife
- Contention (Contention: heated disagreements[2])
- Hatred
- Anger and rage
- Violence
- Bigotry and racism (Bigotry: intolerance toward those who hold different opinions from oneself[2])
- Vigilantism
- Suppressed anger and rage
- Familiar spirit of jealousy

Break the Stronghold of Jealousy and command all spirits to leave.
Bless them with the love of God.

And walk in love, just as Christ also loved you and gave Himself up for us, an offering and a sacrifice to God as a fragrant aroma. (Ephesians 5:2)

STRONGHOLD OF LYING

"Therefore look! The LORD has put a lying spirit in the mouth of these prophets of yours, and the LORD has declared disaster against you." (2 Chronicles 18:22)

Lying: the act of being dishonest, untrue, or false.

Prayer:

I renounce the Stronghold of Lying and its manifestations and fruit.

I repent of and renounce:
- Strong deception
- Self-deception
- False prophecies and word curses
- Gossip
- Flattery
- Exaggeration
- False memories
- Lies from false teachers
- All lies ("white" and "black")
- Slander
- Accusations
- Religious bondages
- Superstitions and old wives' tales
- Profanity
- Guilt (shame and condemnation)
- Homosexuality (also bisexuality and lesbianism)
- A melancholy spirit
- False burdens
- Breaking covenant
- A familiar spirit of lying

Break the Stronghold of Lying and command all spirits to leave.
Bless them with the Spirit of truth (Jesus).

> *". . . that is the Spirit of truth, whom the world cannot receive, because it does not see Him or know Him, but you know Him because He abides with you and will be in you."* (John 14:17)

> *"When the Helper comes, whom I will send to you from the Father, that is the Spirit of truth who proceeds from the Father, He will testify about Me."* (John 15:26)

> *"But when He, the Spirit of truth, comes, He will guide you into all the truth; for He will not speak on His own initiative, but whatever He hears, He will speak; and He will disclose to you what is to come."* (John 16:13)

STRONGHOLD OF PERVERSION

The Lord has mingled a perverse spirit in her midst. (Isaiah 19:14)

Perversion: the alteration of something from its original course, meaning or state to a distortion or corruption of what was first intended (i.e., wisdom and truth being perverted). Also a sexual behavior or desire considered abnormal or unacceptable.[2]

Prayer:
I renounce the Stronghold of Perversion and its manifestations and fruit.

I repent of and renounce:
- Lying
- A broken spirit
- Uncleanness and lewdness
- Evil actions
- Abortion
- Child abuse and molestation
- Incest—physical and emotional
- Prostitution (body, soul, spirit)
- Masturbation and self-gratification
- Exposure and voyeurism (Exposure: the act of making visible a body part, especially the genitals or breasts, in public or in a manner that is illegal or inappropriate. Voyeur: a person who derives sexual gratification from observing the sexual acts of others.[5])
- Atheism
- Filthy mindedness
- Sex perversions
- Doctrinal error
- Twisting the Word
- Satanic ritual abuse
- Ritual molestation and rape
- Satanic dedications and marriage ceremonies
- Rape
- Sodomy
- Pornography
- Chronic worry
- Selfishness
- Egocentric thinking
- Contentiousness and foolishness
- Lust
- Homosexuality and lesbianism
- Bisexualism and bestiality
- S & M (Sadomasochism: sexual arousal involving violence and distress)
- Vain imagination and fantasy lust

- Frigid spirit (sexual or emotional) (Frigid sexually—unable or unwilling to be sexually aroused and responsive.[2] Frigid emotionally—showing no friendliness or enthusiasm; stiff or formal in behavior or style.[2])
- Effeminate spirit (male) (Effeminate: having traits, tastes, habits that are traditionally considered feminine[6])
- Masculine spirit (female) (Masculine: having qualities traditionally ascribed to men[6])
- Fornication and adultery
- All sexual demons, including:
  - Incubus (demonic sexual attacks on women)
  - Succubus (demonic sexual attacks on men)
- Familiar spirit of perversion

Break the Stronghold of Perversion and command all spirits to leave.
Bless them with God's Spirit, purity, and holiness.

> *Now may the God of peace Himself sanctify you entirely; and may your spirit and soul and body be preserved complete, without blame at the coming of our Lord Jesus Christ.* (1 Thessalonians 5:23)

STRONGHOLD OF A SEDUCING SPIRIT

Now the Spirit expressly says that in latter times some will depart from the faith, giving heed to deceiving [seducing] spirits and doctrines of demons. (1 Timothy 4:1)

Seduce: to attract or lead (someone) away from proper behavior or thinking.[5]

Prayer:

I renounce the Stronghold of Seducing and Deceiving Spirits and their manifestations and fruit.

I repent of and renounce:
- A seared conscience
- All deception
- A vigilante spirit
- All fascination with:
  - Evil ways
  - Evil objects
  - Evil persons
- Seducers and enticers
- Wandering from the truth
- Manipulation and control
- Hypocritical lies
- All attraction to and fascination with:
  - False prophets
  - Signs and wonders, etc.
- A Jezebel spirit (divisiveness, control, and witchcraft)
- An Ahab spirit (complacency)
- Familiar spirit of seduction

Break the Stronghold of a Seducing Spirit and command all spirits to leave.
Bless them with the Holy Spirit of truth.

> *"But when He, the Spirit of truth, comes, He will guide you into all the truth; for He will not speak on His own initiative, but whatever He hears, He will speak; and He will disclose to you what is to come." (John 16:13)*

STRONGHOLD OF STUPOR

"God gave them a spirit of stupor, eyes to see not and ears to hear not, down to this very day." (Romans 11:8)

Stupor: a condition of greatly dulled or completely suspended sense or sensibility.[4]

Prayer:

I renounce the Stronghold of the Spirit of Stupor and its manifestations and fruit.

I repent of and renounce:
- Having a form of godliness, but denying its power
- Pride
- Religious legalism
- Spiritual blindness
- Spiritual deafness
- Unbelief
- Complacency
- Deception
- Stubbornness/hardness of heart
- Lethargy
- Dullness of comprehension

Break the Stronghold of Stupor and command all spirits to leave.
Bless them with the Holy Spirit and gifts.

> *But to each one is given the manifestation of the Spirit for the common good. For to one is given the word of wisdom through the Spirit, and to another the word of knowledge according to the same Spirit; to another faith by the same Spirit, and to another gifts of healing by the one Spirit, and to another the effecting of miracles, and to another prophecy, and to another the distinguishing of spirits, to another various kinds of tongues, and to another the interpretation of tongues. But one and the same Spirit works all these things, distributing to each one individually just as He wills. For even as the body is one and yet has many members, and all the members of the body, though they are many, are one body, so also is Christ.*
> (1 Corinthians 12:7–12)

Notes

1. Based on the sixteen strongholds from *Strongman's His Name... What's His Game?: An Authoritative Biblical Approach to Spiritual Warfare* (new edition) by Drs. Jerry & Carol Robeson. Copyright © 1984 by Jerry (Gerald) and Carol Robeson. Used by permission of Whitaker House. www.whitakerhouse.com

2. *Oxford Dictionaries Online*. S.v. "atonement," S.v. "death," S.v. "error," S.v. "fear," S.v. "haughtiness," S.v. "obstinate," S.v. "domineer," S.v. "dissention," S.v. "jealousy," S.v. "contention," S.v. "bigotry," S.v. "perversion," S.v. "frigid." Accessed October 19, 2018, https://en.oxforddictionaries.com

3. *Baker's Evangelical Dictionary of Biblical Theology.* Edited by Walter A. Elwell. Copyright © 1996 by Walter A. Elwell. Published by Baker Books, a division of Baker Book House Company, Grand Rapids, Michigan USA.

4. *Merriam-Webster.com*. "Bondage," "Divination," "Stupor." Accessed October 18, 2018, https://www.merriam-webster.com

5. *American Heritage® Dictionary of the English Language, Fifth Edition*. S.v. «exposure," S.v. "voyeur," S.v. "seduce." Retrieved October 19 2018 from https://www.thefreedictionary.com

6. *Random House Kernerman Webster's College Dictionary*. S.v. "effeminate," S.v. "masculine." Retrieved October 19 2018 from https://www.thefreedictionary.com

APPENDIX 1
PRE- AND POST-MINISTRY FORMS

The forms in this appendix are used in the application/interview process and after deliverance ministry is completed. They can be copied as needed for the purpose of deliverance ministry in accordance with the training in this manual. The completed forms should be kept on file.

- *Deliverance Ministry Questionnaire* (pre-ministry)
  This questionnaire is used for the purpose of gathering much-needed information to help determine the ministry needs of the applicant. This information helps identify potential access points for the formation of spiritual strongholds. The ministry director should adequately review the information before an interview is scheduled.

- *Release and Waiver* SAMPLE (pre-ministry)
  Consult local laws and appropriate legal counsel for your country/territory and ministry. This form does not constitute legal advice and is provided as an *example* of the sort of release form the recipient should sign before receiving deliverance ministry.

- *Deliverance Session Report* (post-ministry)
  After each ministry session the team leader completes this form, with input from each team member, to provide a summary and necessary information for any follow-up sessions.

- *Deliverance Ministry Feedback* (post-ministry)
  The ministry recipient completes this form after the completion of all ministry sessions. It can be taken home and returned by the recipient at a later time.

DELIVERANCE MINISTRY QUESTIONNAIRE[1]

Confidential Information

Name: _____ Today's Date: _____

Address: _____

Phone: _____ Email _____

Age: _____ Birthday: _____ Staff Status _____

Male _____ Female _____ Spiritual Counselor: _____

Marital Status: Single   Married   Divorced   Remarried   Widowed

Please briefly answer the following:

1. What is your church background? Denomination(s) and/or church experience.

2. When did you accept Jesus Christ into your life? _____
   Briefly describe your conversion experience:

3. Was your life really changed?   Yes   No

   If so, how?

4. Have you been baptized since your conversion?   Yes   No

   If yes, when? _____

5. Do you have assurance of salvation?   Yes   No

   If no, please explain:

6. Have you been filled with the Holy Spirit?   Yes   No

   If yes, when _____, and what is the evidence you have
   seen?

7. Describe the content and frequency of your personal devotion and prayer time:

8. Where were you born? (city, state, nation) _____, _____, _____

9. Have you lived in other countries? Yes No

   If yes, which ones?

10. Have you traveled to other countries? Yes No

    If yes, which ones?

Family Background and Relationships (circle all answers that apply)

11. Where was your father born? (city, state, nation) _____, _____, _____

12. Where was your mother born? (city, state, nation) _____, _____, _____

13. Were you a planned child? Yes No Don't know

14. Were you the "right sex?" Yes No Don't know

15. Were you conceived out of wedlock? Yes No Don't know

16. Were you adopted? Yes No Don't know
    If yes, at what age? _____
    If yes, do you know your natural parents? Yes No

17. Was your mother in trauma during pregnancy with you? Yes No Don't know

18. Were you "bonded at birth?" Yes No Don't know

19. Are your parents living? Father Yes No
    Mother Yes No

    If no, how old were you when they died? _____

20. Are your parents Christians? Father Yes No Don't know
    Mother Yes No Don't know

21. In whose home(s) were you raised?
    ___ Both biological parents' home   ___ Adoptive parent's   ___ Mother's home
    ___ Father's home   ___ Grandparent's home   ___ Orphanage
    ___ Foster home(s)   ___ Friend's home   ___ Other relative's home

22. Were you raised in a Christian home? Yes No

23. Was (is) your father:
    Passive   Strong and Manipulative   Neither
    Would you say you had a good relationship with your father? Yes No
    Would your father say you had a good relationship with him? Yes No Don't know

Briefly describe your past and present relationship with your father:

24. Was (is) your mother:
      Passive   Strong and Manipulative   Neither
    Would you say you had a good relationship with your mother?   Yes   No
    Would your mother say you had a good relationship with her?   Yes   No   Don't know
    Briefly describe your past and present relationship with your mother:

25. Was your upbringing in an alcoholic or drug-dominated home?   Yes   No
    If yes, please briefly explain:

26. Do you have brothers or sisters?   Yes   No
    Names: 1. _____ Age _____ brother/sister/full/half/step
                  2. _____ Age _____ brother/sister/full/half/step
                  3. _____ Age _____ brother/sister/full/half/step
                  4. _____ Age _____ brother/sister/full/half/step
                  5. _____ Age _____ brother/sister/full/half/step
                  6. _____ Age _____ brother/sister/full/half/step
                                                            (circle all that apply)

27. Where did you fall in the sibling line? _____

28. Briefly describe your relationship with your siblings while you were growing up:

29. Briefly describe your relationship with your siblings today:

30. Was yours a happy home during childhood?   Yes   No

31. Were you lonely as a teenager?   Yes   No
    Briefly explain:

32. How would you describe your family's financial situation when you were a child?
    ____ Poor   ____ Below average   ____ Average   ____ Above average   ____ Highly affluent

33. Was (is) your father a perfectionist?   Yes   No

34. Was (is) your mother a perfectionist?   Yes   No

35. Were you raised in a physically or verbally abusive home?   Yes   No
    If yes, please briefly explain:

36. Were you sexually abused at home?   Yes   No
    If yes, please briefly explain:

37. Were you ever sexually abused outside the home?   Yes   No
    If yes, please briefly explain:

38. Have you, your spouse, your parents, or your grandparents been in any of the following cults?

    ____ Occultism   ____ Rosicrucian
    ____ Jehovah's Witnesses   ____ Gurus
    ____ Unity   ____ Spiritism / Spiritualist churches
    ____ Children of Love   ____ Christadelphians
    ____ Scientology   ____ Baha'i
    ____ Religious communes   ____ Theosophy
    ____ Native religions   ____ Unification Church
    ____ Islam   ____ Hinduism
    ____ Buddhism   ____ Christian Science
    ____ Mormons

    Others _____

    If you have checked any of the above, state who, what, when, and to what extent:

39. Have you, your spouse, your parents, or your grandparents been a member of any of the following?

    ____ Freemasons (Masonic Lodges)   ____ Oddfellows
    ____ Rainbow Girls   ____ Ku Klux Klan
    ____ Eastern Star   ____ Shriners
    ____ Elks Club   ____ DeMolay
    ____ Job's Daughters   ____ Daughters of the Nile
    ____ Others _____

    If you have checked any of the above, state who, what, when and to what extent:

40. Have you, your spouse, your parents, or your grandparents suffered from any of the following:

____ High fever	____ Arthritis	____ Cancer
____ Viral infections	____ Asthma	____ Hay fever
____ Allergies	____ Impotence	____ Bent body
____ Multiple sclerosis	____ Muscular dystrophy	____ Diabetes
____ Blindness	____ Blood disease	____ Lingering disorders
____ Mental problems	____ Alcoholism	____ Drug use
____ Rx tranquilizers		

Others _____

If you have checked any of the above, state who, what, when and to what extent:

41 Did either of your parents suffer from depression?   Father   Mother   Neither

If you circled *Mother* or *Father*, describe their depression and its impact at home:

This is about you:

42. Are you easily frustrated?   Yes   No
    If yes, do you show it or bury it?   Show   Bury
    If yes, state what frustrates you:

43. Would you describe yourself as: Anxious   Yes   No
                                       A worrier   Yes   No
                                       Depressed   Yes   No

44. Have you personally ever had psychiatric counseling?   Yes   No

    When? _____

45. Have you ever been hypnotized?   Yes   No

46. Do you feel mentally confused?   Yes   No

47. Do you daydream or have mental fantasies?   Yes   No

48. Do you suffer from frequent bad dreams/nightmares?   Yes   No
    Describe any recurring theme:

49. Have you ever been tempted to commit suicide?   Yes   No
    If yes, when and why?

50. Have you tried to commit suicide?   Yes   No

    If yes, how, when, and why?

51. Have you ever wished to die?   Yes   No

52. Have you been involved in occultism or witchcraft?   Yes   No

53. Have you ever had involvement with any of the following?
    - ____ Fortune tellers   ____ Tarot cards   ____ Ouija boards
    - ____ Séances   ____ Mediums   ____ Palmistry
    - ____ Astrology   ____ Color therapy   ____ Levitation
    - ____ Astral travel   ____ Horoscopes   ____ Lucky charms
    - ____ Black magic   ____ White magic   ____ Demon worship
    - ____ Spirit guides   ____ Clairvoyance   ____ Crystals
    - ____ Automatic handwriting ____ Native healer   ____ Dungeons & Dragons
    - ____ New Age movement   ____ Witch doctors   ____ Voodoo

    Others _____

    Describe your involvement with any of the above:

54. Have you ever read books on occultism or witchcraft?   Yes   No
    If yes, what and why?

55. Have you made any pacts with Satan?   Yes   No
    If yes, what?

56. Do you know of any curse placed on you or your family?   Yes   No
    If yes, when, by whom, and why?

57. Have you been involved in Transcendental Meditation?   Yes   No

58. Have you been involved in Eastern religions?   Yes   No

59. Have you ever visited heathen temples?   Yes   No

60. Have you ever done any form of yoga?   Yes   No

61. Have you learned/used mind communication or mind control?   Yes   No

62. Have you ever seen a demonic presence?   Yes   No
    If yes, briefly explain:

63. Do you currently have in your home any symbols of idols or spirit worship, such as:
    ____ Buddhas   ____ Totem poles   ____ Painted facemasks
    ____ Idol carvings   ____ Fetish objects or feathers ____ Pagan symbols
    ____ Tikis   ____ Native art   ____ Kachina dolls

64. What type of music did you occupy your mind with before conversion?
    ____ Rock & roll   ____ Punk rock   ____ New Age
    ____ Rap   ____ Heavy metal   ____ Country
    ____ Gospel/Christian   ____ Classical   ____ Contemporary

65. What type of music do you occupy your mind with now?
    ____ Rock & roll   ____ Punk rock   ____ New Age
    ____ Rap   ____ Heavy metal   ____ Country
    ____ Gospel/Christian   ____ Classical   ____ Contemporary

66. Have you ever learned any of the martial arts?   Yes   No
    If yes, describe and explain:

67. Have you ever had premonitions, déjà vu, or psychic sight?   Yes   No
    If yes, describe and explain:

68. Do you have any tattoos?   Yes   No

69. Have you ever utilized any of the following drugs:
    ____ LSD   ____ Speed   ____ Marijuana
    ____ Cocaine   ____ Crack   ____ Uppers
    ____ Downers   ____ Other drugs
    Others: _____
    Were you addicted?   Yes   No

70. Have you been addicted to any of the following:
    ____ Gambling   ____ Compulsive exercise   ____ Wasteful spending
    ____ Television   ____ Alcohol   ____ Smoking
    ____ Food   ____ Coffee   ____ Shopping
    ____ Pornography   ____ Sex   ____ Medical prescriptions
    Drugs _____

For questions 71 through 86 please place a "P" for past, a "C" for current, or "PC" for both.

71. In your Christian experience do you:

    ____ Have trouble accepting the deity of Christ
    ____ Have trouble accepting the teachings of Christ
    ____ Tend to gravitate toward humanistic thinking
    ____ Not believe you have an anointing on your life
    ____ Seem to always be persecuted in your walk with Christ

    ____ Tend to unknowingly suppress ministries
    ____ Tend to have a lawlessness about you
    ____ Tend to often be in heretical teaching
    ____ Have trouble accepting God's forgiveness
    ____ Have trouble accepting Christ's atoning sacrifice

72. I have in the past or currently struggle with the following:

    ____ Lust
    ____ Various forms of corruption
    ____ Fear of death
    ____ Oppression
    ____ Controlling
    ____ A bound mind

    ____ Satanic interest
    ____ My ambitions and achievements
    ____ Bitterness
    ____ Spiritual blindness
    ____ Religion
    ____ Spiritual deadness

73. I have in the past or currently experience problems in the following areas:

    ____ Mental illness
    ____ Near drowning experience
    ____ Crippled
    ____ Foaming at the mouth
    ____ Gnashing of teeth
    ____ Burned
    ____ Prostration
    ____ Self-mutilation
    ____ Insanity
    ____ Senility
    ____ Seizures
    ____ Paranoia
    ____ Hallucinations
    ____ Attention deficit

    ____ Ear problems
    ____ Spiritual deafness or blindness
    ____ Excessive crying or tearing
    ____ Alzheimer's
    ____ Pining away
    ____ Chemical imbalance
    ____ Suicidal
    ____ Madness
    ____ Retardation
    ____ Schizophrenia
    ____ Epilepsy
    ____ Hear voices
    ____ Palsy
    ____ Eating disorders:

    Type(s) _____

74. I have in the past or currently experience problems in the following areas:

    ____ Death seems to be lurking nearby
    ____ Suicide
    ____ Fighting
    ____ Death to ministry
    ____ Death in marriage
    ____ Random acts of violence

    ____ Disease
    ____ Clumsiness
    ____ Dare devil acts
    ____ Death in relationships
    ____ Accidents

75. I have in the past or currently experience interest in the following areas:

____ Divination	____ False prophecy
____ Fortune telling or soothsayers	____ Stargazing, zodiac, horoscopes
____ Rebellion	____ Hypnotists / enchanters
____ Acupuncture	____ Birth charts
____ Magic (black or white)	____ Spiritists
____ Self will	____ Mind control / manipulation
____ Warlocks	____ Witches
____ Sorcerers	____ Wizards
____ Spirit guides	____ Vampires
____ Animal guides	____ Astral projection
____ Water witching	____ Lust for power or control

76. I have in the past or currently struggle with the following areas:

____ Error in doctrine	____ False Prophecy
____ An unsubmissive attitude	____ Hyperspirituality
____ Twisting of scripture	____ Unteachable spirit
____ Mixing the holy with the profane	____ Defensiveness
____ Argumentative	____ New Age movement
____ Contentiousness	____ Servant to corruption
____ Maintaining a form of godliness	____ Mental confusion
____ Fears	____ Dullness of comprehension
____ Hindrances to prayer	____ Hindrances to Bible study
____ Hindrances to hearing sermons	____ Hindrances to movement of the Holy Spirit
____ Hindrances to believing faith principles	
____ False doctrines within Mormonism, Catholicism, Buddhism, Hinduism, Unitarianism	

77. I am or have in the past been involved in the following areas:

____ Familiar spirits	____ Divination
____ Witchcraft	____ Calling on mediums
____ Yoga	____ Clairvoyance
____ Inferiority	____ Mind dreaming
____ Spirit guides / animal guides	____ False prophecy
____ Séances	____ Bigotry
____ Racism	____ Low self-esteem
____ Peeping and muttering	____ Self pity
____ Necromancy	____ Drugs (illegal or prolonged use of legal)

78. I have in the past or currently struggle with the following:

____ Fear	____ Torment / horror
____ Fear of death	____ A desire to be a hermit or recluse
____ Anxiety / stress	____ Extroversion
____ Fear of saying no	____ Introversion
____ Fear of heights	____ Worry / doubt / lack of trust
____ Migraines	____ Fear of rejection

    ____ Fear of abandonment   ____ Fear of spiders
    ____ Panic attacks   ____ Fear of heart attacks
    ____ Fear of authority   ____ Fear of failure
    ____ A constant desire to be alone   ____ A critical spirit
    ____ Unhealthy fear of God   ____ Fear of not being good enough
    ____ Fear of animals
    ____ Other fears (list): _____

79. I have in the past or currently struggle with the following:
    - ____ Haughtiness   ____ Religious pride
    - ____ Rationalizing pride   ____ Scornful attitude
    - ____ Vanity   ____ Professional pride
    - ____ Regional pride   ____ Obstinate
    - ____ National pride   ____ Self righteous
    - ____ Dictatorial   ____ Controlling
    - ____ Overbearing or domineering   ____ Manipulative
    - ____ Rejection of God's authority   ____ Rejection of man's authority
    - ____ Rebellion   ____ A holier-than-thou attitude
    - ____ Exalted feelings   ____ Gossip
    - ____ Egotistical attitude   ____ Self-deception
    - ____ Contentiousness   ____ Bragging and boastful attitude
    - ____ Strife   ____ Idleness
    - ____ Performance orientation   ____ Attention seeking
    - ____ Interrupting others   ____ Impatience
    - ____ "Always right" attitude   ____ Being arrogant and smug

80. I have in the past or currently struggle with the following areas:
    - ____ Self hate   ____ Self pity
    - ____ A broken heart   ____ Many regrets
    - ____ Inner hurts and a torn spirit   ____ Gluttony
    - ____ Loneliness   ____ Dejection
    - ____ Continuous sorrow and grief   ____ Discouragement
    - ____ Despair   ____ Hopelessness
    - ____ Rejection   ____ Insecurity
    - ____ Abandonment   ____ Inferiority
    - ____ Life's unfairness   ____ Suicidal thoughts
    - ____ Depression   ____ Excessive mourning
    - ____ Insomnia   ____ False responsibility
    - ____ Low self-esteem   ____ Suppressed emotions

81. I have in the past or currently suffer from the following infirmities:
    - ____ Infirmity in general   ____ Bent body / spine
    - ____ Chemical imbalance   ____ Extended fever
    - ____ Impotence   ____ Frailness
    - ____ Lameness   ____ Arthritis

____ Diabetes
____ Tuberculosis
____ Excessive pain and affliction
____ Tumors
____ Warts
____ Viral infections
____ Asthma
____ Allergies
____ Seizures
____ Hypochondria
____ Cancer—list type(s): _____

____ Oppression
____ Emphysema
____ Lingering disorders
____ Cysts
____ Excessive fatigue
____ Bacterial infections
____ Hay fever
____ Epilepsy
____ Leukemia

82. I have in the past or currently struggle with the following:
____ Jealousy
____ Spite
____ Extreme competition
____ Coveting
____ Envy
____ Contentiousness
____ Anger and rage
____ Bigotry and racism
____ Suppressed rage

____ Revenge
____ Cruelty
____ Causing divisions
____ Selfishness
____ Strife
____ Hatred
____ Violence
____ Suppressed anger
____ Desire to murder

83. I have in the past or continue to struggle with the following:
____ Lying
____ Driving zeal
____ False prophecy
____ Exaggeration
____ Slander
____ Religious bondage
____ Superstitions
____ Guilt
____ Condemnation
____ Self deception
____ Frenzied emotional actions

____ Flattery
____ Strong deception
____ Gossip
____ False teaching
____ Accusations
____ Covenant breaking
____ Profanity
____ Shame
____ Melancholy nature
____ False burdens

84. I have in the past or continue to struggle with the following:
____ Perversity
____ Evil actions
____ Child abuse
____ Masturbation
____ A filthy mind
____ Doctrinal error
____ Molestation

____ Broken spirit
____ Past abortion
____ Prostitution
____ Atheism
____ Sexual perversions
____ Twisting the Word
____ Incest

____ Rape
____ Spousal rape
____ Computer pornography
____ Self lover
____ Foolishness
____ Homosexuality
____ Vain imaginations
____ Sexual frigidity
____ Effeminate spirit
____ Adultery

____ Date rape
____ Pornography
____ Chronic worrying
____ Contentiousness
____ Lust
____ Lesbianism
____ Rebellion
____ Emotional frigidity
____ Fornication

85. I have in the past or continue to struggle with the following:
    ____ Seducing spirits
    ____ Deception
    ____ Seducers
    ____ Fascination with evil objects
    ____ Hypocritical lies
    ____ Attracted to false signs
    ____ Attracted to false wonders
    ____ Ahab spirit (passivity)

    ____ Seared conscience
    ____ Fascination with evil ways
    ____ Enticers
    ____ Wandering from the truth
    ____ Fascination with evil people
    ____ Attracted to false prophets
    ____ Jezebel spirit

86. I have in the past or continue to struggle with the following:
    ____ Addiction to entertainment
    ____ Adultery
    ____ Love of money
    ____ Worldliness
    ____ Idolatry
    ____ Love of self
    ____ Addiction to sports

    ____ Unfaithfulness
    ____ Prostitution of spirit, soul, or body
    ____ Excessive appetite
    ____ Fornication
    ____ Chronic dissatisfaction
    ____ Self reward
    ____ Addiction to television

87. Please describe as clearly as you can what is going on in your life at this time. What was it that prompted you to seek spiritual counseling?

What do I think?
Please place a check by each statement that describes your thinking about yourself!

88. ____ I am all alone.
    ____ They do not need me.
    ____ No one ever cares.
    ____ God has forsaken me too.
    ____ No one will believe me.
    ____ I am afraid they won't come back.

    ____ I have been overlooked.
    ____ I don't matter.
    ____ They are not coming back.
    ____ There is no one to protect me.
    ____ I cannot trust anyone.

89. ____ I am so stupid, ignorant, an idiot.
    ____ I was a participant.
    ____ I should have done something to have stopped it from happening.
    ____ I should have told someone.
    ____ I felt pleasure so I must have wanted it.
    ____ It happened because of my looks, my gender, my body, etc.
    ____ I did not try to run away.
    ____ I deserved it.
    ____ I did it to him/her first.
    ____ I allowed it.
    ____ I should have known better.
    ____ It was my fault.
    ____ I knew what was going to happen yet I stayed anyway.
    ____ I was a participant.
    ____ I should have stopped them.
    ____ I am cheap like a slut.
    ____ I was paid for service rendered.
    ____ I kept going back.
    ____ I'm bad, dirty, shameful, sick, nasty.

90. ____ I am going to die.
    ____ If I tell, they will come back and hurt me.
    ____ If I trust, I will die.
    ____ It is just a matter of time before it happens again.
    ____ They are going to get me.
    ____ Something bad will happen if I tell / stop it / confront it.
    ____ He/she is going to hurt me.
    ____ I do not know what to do.
    ____ He/she/they are coming back.
    ____ If I let him/her/them into my life they will hurt me too.
    ____ Doom is just around the corner.

91. ____ He/she/they are too strong to resist.
    ____ I am going to die, and I cannot do anything about it.
    ____ The pain is too great to bear.
    ____ I cannot get loose.
    ____ I don't know what to do.
    ____ I'm pulled from every direction.
    ____ I am too small to do anything.
    ____ I cannot stop this.
    ____ There is no way out.
    ____ I am too weak to resist.
    ____ I cannot get away.
    ____ I am overwhelmed.
    ____ Everything is out of control.
    ____ Not even God can help me.

92. ____ I am dirty / evil / shameful / perverted because of what happened to me.
    ____ I will never be happy.
    ____ I will always be unclean / filthy.
    ____ I will always be hurt / damaged / broken
    ____ God could never want me after what has happened to me.
    ____ My life is ruined.
    ____ No one will be able to really love me.
    ____ Everyone can see my shame / filth / dirtiness, etc.
    ____ My body parts are dirty.
    ____ I will never feel clean again.

93. ____ I am not loved, needed, cared for, or important.
    ____ I am worthless and have no value.
    ____ I was a mistake.
    ____ I was never liked by them, because I was _____!
    ____ I am in the way; I am a burden.
    ____ I could never jump high enough to please him/her.
    ____ They do not need me.
    ____ I am unimportant.
    ____ I should have never been born.
    ____ God could never love or accept me.
    ____ I could never be as_____ as him/her.
    ____ I am not acceptable.

94. ____ It is never going to get any better.   ____ There is no way out.
    ____ It will just happen again and again.   ____ There is no good thing for me.
    ____ I have no reason to live.   ____ There are no options for me.
    ____ I just want to die.   ____ Nothing good will ever come of this.

95. ____ I do not know what is happening to me.   ____ Everything is confusing.
    ____ This does not make any sense.   ____ Why would they do this to me?

Other Areas of Your Life

96. Do you have known sin, unforgiveness, resentment, bitterness, or hatred toward anyone? (List all and use another page if needed.) Toward whom and why: _____

    _____
    _____
    _____
    _____
    _____
    _____

97. Have you attended any spiritual counseling programs (such as Living Waters, Foundations, etc.)?
    Yes   No

    If yes, please state which one and where? _____

    The month and year of the retreat/program: Month _____ Year _____

    Please describe your experience:

    _____
    _____
    _____
    _____
    _____

98. Have you received prayer for deliverance?   Yes   No

    If yes, describe your experience:

    _____
    _____
    _____
    _____
    _____

99. Describe your dreams, your goals, and aspirations for your life.

100. Are there any other problems you feel this questionnaire has not addressed?

　　　Please explain:

101. Are you currently taking any medication? If so, what?

102. If there is anything that either was not addressed, or your experience was too sensitive to write about, please describe the experience here or feel free to bring it up at the time of your interview.

Note

[1] Questionnaire reprinted from *Deliverance Training Manual*, William Sudduth and Judith Sudduth (Stephens City, VA: RAM Inc., 2000). Used by permission.

SAMPLE

RELEASE AND WAIVER

(Neither this sample Release Form nor any other statements contained in this book are legal advice. Always seek legal counsel from a competent attorney in your area.)

For and in consideration of the prayer, deliverance, prophetic or other ministry services provided by a ministry team (the "Ministry Team") from _____ (ministry name), I, the undersigned, being legally competent and fully authorized and empowered to do so, do hereby voluntarily and absolutely release, discharge, waive, and relinquish _____ (ministry name) and its officers, agents, servants, or employees, from any and all loss, damages, injuries, claims or causes of action on account of any and all known and unknown personal injuries, mental anguish, and damage claims to person or property resulting from, arising out of, or otherwise related to ministerial services provided by _____ (ministry name) and its agents, representatives and/or employees in any way affecting me.

I understand that the Ministry Team will not be functioning as licensed or professional counselors, ordained and/or full-time ministers, pastors, or counselors (even though some may be licensed and/or ordained as such). I expressly acknowledge that the ministry services provided by _____ (ministry name) will be in accordance with Biblical principles and precepts, and will be conducted according to the guidelines and policies adopted by _____ (ministry name), whether or not these policies are set out or stated.

I further acknowledge that the ministry services provided by _____ (ministry name) are primarily spiritual in nature and are not intended as a substitute for medical treatment, legal services or law enforcement protection, where appropriate. I fully understand that the members of the Ministry Team are in no way attempting to diagnose or treat any medical or psychological condition, or any other act which may constitute the practice of medicine in this state.

I understand, am aware of, and assume all risks inherent in participating in the ministry services of _____ (ministry name). These risks include, but are not limited to, physical and emotional responses and reactions I may experience as a result of this ministry.

I further understand that while the Ministry Team is committed to respecting the sensitive nature of information disclosed during the ministry services, it does not guarantee complete confidentiality. The information, as needed, may be shared with other leaders of _____ (ministry name), as well as those I consider to be my spiritual leadership. This may include future meetings with spiritual mentors to set appropriate boundaries for personal and spiritual growth. Additionally, the law may impose certain reporting obligations upon the Ministry Team in which some types of information must be reported to appropriate authorities. The types of information that may require disclosure include, but are not necessarily limited to, any harm or potential harm that a person may attempt or desire to do to himself/herself or to others, as well as any reasonable suspicion of physical or sexual abuse that has been done or that is being done to a minor child.

I further agree to indemnify and hold harmless _____ (ministry name), its board of directors, officers, agents, servants, or employees, from any and all claims, losses and damages of every kind to any person or property arising out of or attributed to the spiritual, psychological, physical, financial and/or emotional problems for which I am seeking ministry from _____ (ministry name).

I further understand and agree that this waiver and release constitutes an admission and acknowledgment by me that I have received no warranty, guarantee, or promise of any particular result either expressed or implied, from _____ (ministry name), its officers, agents, servants, or employees.

I have signed this disclaimer, waiver and release for myself and with the express intent that it applies to my personal representatives, assigns, heirs, executors, administrators, spouse, or next of kin.

Signature: _____ Date: _____
(Recipient of ministry)
Printed Name: _____

If recipient of ministry is a minor:

Signature: _____ Date: _____
(Parent or Guardian)
Printed Name: _____

DELIVERANCE SESSION REPORT

(Optional/recommended for use by the ministry team leader with input from team members.)

Confidential Information

Ministry Recipient: _____ Place of Ministry: _____

Date: _____

Deliverance Team Leader: _____

Ministering Team Members: _____

_____

Strongholds addressed in this session:

- ☐ Antichrist
- ☐ Bondage
- ☐ Deaf and dumb spirit
- ☐ Death
- ☐ Divination
- ☐ Error
- ☐ Fear
- ☐ Harlotry

- ☐ Haughtiness
- ☐ Heaviness
- ☐ Infirmity
- ☐ Jealousy
- ☐ Lying
- ☐ Perversion
- ☐ Seducing spirit
- ☐ Stupor

Other areas covered in this session:

- ☐ Prayer of Submission to the Lordship of Jesus Christ
- ☐ Forgiveness
- ☐ Soul ties
- ☐ Generational curses
- ☐ Freemasonry
- ☐ Witchcraft
- ☐ Prayer of Blessing

Comments: _____

_____

_____

_____

_____

Team Assessments/Observations

Key observations:
_____
_____
_____
_____
_____
_____
_____

Possible hindrances:
_____
_____
_____
_____
_____

Possible areas to be addressed:
_____
_____
_____
_____
_____

DELIVERANCE MINISTRY FEEDBACK

Name: _____ **Date of ministry:** _____

1. Have you ever received deliverance ministry before? (Y/N)
   If so, how was this ministry different than what you have experienced before?
   _____
   _____
   _____
   _____

2. What did you like/dislike about the way you were ministered to?
   _____
   _____
   _____
   _____

3. Do you feel like this ministry was beneficial to you and your walk with the Lord? (Y/N)
   If no, please explain why not:
   _____
   _____
   _____
   _____

4. Would you recommend this ministry to others? (Y/N)
   Why or why not?
   _____
   _____
   _____
   _____

5. Any other comments:
   _____
   _____
   _____
   _____

APPENDIX 2
PRE- AND POST-MINISTRY HANDOUTS

The following handouts can be copied as needed and provided to the ministry recipient.

- *Preparation for Receiving Deliverance* (pre-ministry handout)
- *Forgiveness* (pre- or post-ministry handout)
- *Moving Forward after Deliverance* (post-ministry handout)

PREPARATION FOR RECEIVING DELIVERANCE

What Deliverance Is
- Others coming alongside you, to help you engage your will. It is your deliverance. We are there to assist you.
- Rooting out the enemy who has gained access through sin, generational issues, unforgiveness, thought processes, etc.
- A step toward walking in freedom. Deliverance is just one of the steps, along with continuing to resist the enemy and renewing your mind. God delivers in many ways and continues to deliver us on an ongoing basis throughout our lives.

What Deliverance Is Not
- A cure-all or a magic fix. You must walk it out!
- Something done **TO** you. Rather, the team is partnering **WITH** you.

What to Expect
- Compassion—you will not be judged!
- Complete confidentiality—all involved have made a promise of confidentiality.
- To be handled with respect and dignity.

Hindrances to Deliverance
- Continuing in present sin, known or unknown.
- Unwillingness to engage your will—you must line up under the truth of God not the lies of the enemy. You must have a desire and determination to be free.
- Lack of openness and honesty—you must tell us what is going on.
- Unforgiveness issues—if you will not forgive, you will not experience freedom. Go through the handout on forgiveness, which explains:
  - What forgiveness is
  - What forgiveness is not
  - How to forgive

Fasting

Fasting is recommended for the person seeking deliverance as well as the team members who are ministering. Fasting can strengthen our faith in the supernatural power of the Holy Spirit, and in turn help break the power of the enemy. In Mark 9:29, Jesus told His disciples "This kind [of demon] can come out by nothing but prayer and fasting" (NKJV), so we recommend team members fast one day a week and the person seeking deliverance fast at whatever capacity they are able in preparation. Fasting doesn't always have to be specifically food, but anything that would be seen as a sacrifice of focused devotion to the Lord. This may include things such as entertainment, social media, sweets, or whatever the Holy Spirit might lead you to lay down. While food is recommended, we understand that due to medical reasons not everyone can participate in fasting that particular way, and we advise consulting your doctor before beginning a fast.

FORGIVENESS

"For if you forgive men their trespasses, your heavenly Father will also forgive you. But if you do not forgive their trespasses, neither will your Father forgive your trespasses." (Matthew 6:14–15 NKJV)

What Forgiveness Is Not

- ☐ Forgiveness is not saying that what a person did to you is okay. It is not okay. It will never be okay. It was wrong.
- ☐ Forgiveness is not a feeling. It is obedience to God's Word. It is a choice. It is a decision to obey God.
- ☐ Forgiveness is not healing. Forgiveness paves the way or opens the door for healing. If you have forgiven someone and still feel pain, it's because you need to receive your healing. The forgiveness comes first, then the healing.

What Forgiveness Is

- ☐ Forgiveness is a command. One of the biggest mistakes we could ever make is thinking forgiveness is an option. It is not an option; it is a commandment. Forgiveness is releasing the offender to God; it is turning them over to God.

Effective Steps to Forgiving Others

1. Get alone and ask the Lord to show you the people you need to forgive.
2. Write down the names of people you need to forgive. (They may be from seemingly insignificant incidents and/or the recent past or long ago, like the little girl from the third grade, your fifth-grade schoolteacher, etc.)
3. Include yourself (if applicable).
4. Include any angry feelings toward God (if applicable).
5. Go over each name with the Lord and express to Him how they have hurt you.
6. Write down what they did and why you need to forgive them.
7. List whatever feelings you had and the degree to which you felt them. (Example: "I was so angry, I did not care if they fell and hurt themselves—actually, I wish they had." "I wished I could have died because of the humiliation.")
8. Choose to forgive and release them. "Lord, I choose to forgive and release [*name of person*]."
9. Do it. Say, "I forgive them."
10. Write a letter to each person. "I forgive and release you from…" (This step is optional. Not all letters will be sent. These are an act of faith. The Lord will see your sincerity.)
11. Look at yourself in the mirror, and forgive and release yourself from everything that you need to forgive yourself for. Declare to yourself that you are forgiven.
12. Receive and believe that you are forgiven by God. (When ministering to others, look the person in the eyes and declare to them, "You are forgiven.")

MOVING FORWARD AFTER DELIVERANCE

Now that you have completed your time of ministry, here are some tools to help you continue in your journey of freedom.

- Understand that the enemy will try to return, but you have been given everything you need to maintain your freedom without fear.

  Seeing that His divine power has granted to us everything pertaining to life and godliness, through the true knowledge of Him who called us by His own glory and excellence. (2 Peter 1:3)

  You are my hiding place; You preserve me from trouble; You surround me with **songs of deliverance**. (Psalm 32:7)

  I sought the Lord, and He answered me, and **delivered** *me from all my fears.* (Psalm 34:4)

- Daily worship, prayer, meditation on God's Word, and consistent study of God's Word will keep demonic spirits from taking back the ground they have lost.

- Have faith in what the Lord has done and the truth of His love for you.

  He who began a good work in you will perfect it . . . (Philippians 1:6)

- Be confident in the truth of your identity and authority in Jesus Christ.

  For all who are being led by the Spirit of God, these are sons of God. For you have not received a spirit of slavery leading to fear again, but you have received a spirit of adoption as sons by which we cry out, "Abba! Father!" The Spirit Himself testifies with our spirit that we are children of God. (Romans 8:14–16)

  "Behold, I give you the authority to trample on serpents and scorpions, and over all the power of the enemy, and nothing shall by any means hurt you." (Luke 10:19 NKJV)

- Stay connected with or get involved in your local church fellowship. Accountability and ongoing discipleship is crucial to your growth and freedom.

- Try to find other strong believers in Jesus Christ and develop godly friendships. Avoid going back to relationships you know aren't right for you.

- Keep closed all previously open doors to the enemy that might have been revealed in your time of ministry (music, movies, relationships, etc. that you know had negative influences over your life).

- Understand that total deliverance can be a process, and ongoing counseling, emotional healing, and the restoration of your thought patterns can take time. Be patient. Stay faithful.

APPENDIX 3

PRAYER FOR RELEASE FROM FREEMASONRY

These prayers are to be prayed with those who have clearly exhibited the effects of high-level participation or familiar association with the cult known as Freemasonry. Do not use these prayers unless it has been determined to be necessary by the team leader.

Recipient Instructions

If you were once a Mason or are a descendant of a Mason, we recommend that you pray through the following prayer of renunciation of Freemasonry. First, please read through all of it, so you know what you are renouncing and of what you are repenting. Masons are given their oaths one line at a time and without prior knowledge of their commitments and consequences. We want you to be fully aware of the entire process. It is best to pray this aloud with a Christian friend or church leader present.

It is recommended that the person leading the ministry time and the recipient both have copies of the script. The ministry leader can read a short portion of the statement and the recipient can repeat after them. We suggest a brief pause following each paragraph to allow the Holy Spirit to show any additional areas that may require attention and prayer.

INITIAL PRAYERS

Dear Lord Jesus, I believe that You are the Son of God, that You died on the cross for my sins, and that You rose again from the dead. I confess You as my Lord and Savior. I repent of all my sins. I come as a sinner seeking forgiveness and cleansing from all sins committed against You.

I honor my earthly father and mother and all my ancestors of flesh and blood, of the spirit by adoption, and godparents. Yet I repent of and renounce all their sins, unholy covenants, idolatry, and any curses they brought to my family and me. I forgive all my ancestors for the effects of their sins on my spouse, my children, grandchildren, and on me. I confess and renounce all of my own sins. I renounce Satan and every spiritual power of his.

General Renouncing

I renounce and forsake all involvement in Freemasonry or any other Lodge or Craft by my ancestors and myself. I renounce witchcraft, the principal spirit behind Freemasonry, and I renounce Baphomet, the spirit of Antichrist, and the curse of the Luciferian doctrine. I renounce the idolatry, blasphemy, secrecy, and deception of Masonry at every level. I specifically renounce the insecurity, the love of position and power, the love of money, greed, or pride, which may have led my ancestors into Masonry. I renounce all the fears, which held them in Masonry, especially the fear of death, fear of man, and fear of trusting. I renounce all fears caused by Masonry, in the name of Jesus Christ, amen.

I renounce every position held in the Lodge by any of my ancestors, including "Tyler," "Master," "Worshipful Master," and others. I renounce the calling of any man "Master," for Jesus Christ is my only Master and Lord, and He forbids anyone else having that title. I renounce the entrapping of others into Masonry and observing their helplessness during the rituals. I renounce the effects of Masonry passed on to me through any female ancestor who felt distrusted and rejected by her husband as he entered and attended any Lodge and refused to tell her of his secret activities. In Jesus' name, amen.

I renounce the ancient pagan teaching and symbolism of: The First Tracing Board, The Second Tracing Board, and The Third Tracing Board used in the rituals of the Blue Lodge. I renounce the pagan ritual of the "Point within a Circle" with all its bondages and phallus worship.

I renounce the occult mysticism of the black and white mosaic checkered floor with the tessellated border and five-pointed blazing star or sunburst in the center. I renounce the symbol "G" and its veiled pagan symbolism and bondages. I renounce and utterly forsake the Great Architect of the Universe, who is revealed in the higher degrees as Lucifer, and his false claim to be the universal fatherhood of God. I also renounce the false claim that Lucifer is the Morning Star and Shining One and I declare that Jesus Christ is the Bright and Morning Star of Revelation 22:16. In Jesus' name, amen.

I renounce the All-Seeing Third Eye in the forehead (or Horus) and its pagan and occult symbolism. I renounce all false communions taken and the mockery of the redemptive work of Jesus Christ on the cross of Calvary. I renounce all unbelief, confusion, and depression, and renounce all worship of Lucifer as God. I renounce and forsake the lie of Freemasonry that man is not sinful, but merely imperfect, and so can redeem himself through good works. I rejoice that the Bible is true and that I cannot do a single thing to earn my salvation, but that I can only be saved by grace through faith in Jesus Christ and what He accomplished on the cross of Calvary. In Jesus' name, amen.

I renounce all fear of insanity, anguish, death wishes, suicide, and death, in the name of Jesus Christ. Jesus Christ conquered death, and He alone holds the keys of death and hell. I rejoice that He holds my life in His hands now. He came to give me life abundantly and eternally, and I believe His promises.

I renounce all anger, hatred, murderous thoughts, revenge, retaliation, spiritual apathy, and false religions. I renounce all unbelief, especially unbelief in the Holy Bible as God's Word. I renounce all compromise of God's Word. I renounce all spiritual searching into false religions, and all striving to please God. I rest in the knowledge that I have found my Lord and Savior Jesus Christ, and that He has found me.

RENOUNCING THE DEGREES

Entry Levels: Craft Freemasonry: 1°– 3° (Grand Lodge)

1st or Entered Apprentice Degree
I renounce oaths taken and curses involved in the 1st or Entered Apprentice Degree, especially their effects on the throat and tongue. I renounce the Hoodwink, the blindfold, and its effects on my emotions and my eyes, including all confusion, fear of the dark, fear of the light, and fear of sudden noises. I renounce the secret word BOAZ, and all it means. I renounce the mixing and mingling of truth and error, and the blasphemy of this degree of Masonry. I renounce the noose around the neck, the fear of choking, and also every spirit causing asthma, hay fever, allergies, emphysema, or any other breathing difficulty. I renounce the compass point, the sword or spear held against the breast. I renounce the fear of death by stabbing pain, and the fear of heart attack from this degree. In the name of Jesus Christ I now pray for healing of my throat, vocal cords, nasal passages, sinus, bronchial tubes, and for healing of my speech area. I pray for the release of the Word of God to me and through me and my family, in Jesus' name, amen.

2nd or Fellow Craft Degree
I renounce oaths taken and curses involved in the 2nd or Fellow Craft Degree, especially curses on the heart, chest, and lung area. I renounce the secret words JACHIN and SHIBBOLETH and all that these mean. I cut off all emotional hardness, apathy, indifference, unbelief, and deep anger from my family and me. In the name of Jesus Christ I now pray for the healing of my chest, lungs, and heart area, and also for the healing of my emotions. I ask to be made sensitive to the Holy Spirit of God, in Jesus' name, amen.

3rd or Master Mason Degree
I renounce oaths taken and curses involved in the 3rd or Master Mason Degree, especially curses on the stomach and womb area. I renounce the secret words MAHABONE, MACHABEN, MACHBINNA, and TUBAL CAIN, and all they mean. I renounce the Spirit of Death from blows to the head enacted as ritual murder. I renounce the fear of death, false martyrdom, fear of violent gang attack, assault, or rape, and the helplessness of this degree. I renounce the falling into a coffin or stretcher involved in the ritual of murder. I renounce the false resurrection of this degree, because only Jesus Christ is the Resurrection and the Life. I also renounce the blasphemous kissing of the Bible on a witchcraft oath. I cut off all spirits of death, witchcraft, and deception. In the name of Jesus Christ, I now pray for healing of my stomach, gall bladder, womb, liver, and any other organs of my body affected by Masonry. I ask for a release of compassion and understanding for my family and me, in Jesus' name, amen.

York Rite (aka American Rite)

York Rite, The Mark Lodge
I renounce oaths taken and curses involved in the York Rite of Masonry. I renounce the Mark Lodge, and the mark in the form of squares and angles which marks the person for life. I also reject the jewel or talisman, which may have been made from this mark and worn at lodge meetings.

Mark Master Degree
I renounce oaths taken and curses involved in The Mark Master Degree with its secret word JOPPA. I renounce its penalty of having the right ear smote off and the curse of permanent deafness, as well as the right hand being chopped off for being an impostor.

Virtual Past Master Degree
I renounce oaths taken and curses involved in the other York Rite Degrees, including The Virtual Past Master Degree with the penalty of having my tongue split from tip to root.

Most Excellent Master Degree
I renounce oaths taken and curses involved in the Most Excellent Master Degree, with the penalty of having my breast torn open and my heart and vital organs removed and exposed to rot on the dung hill.

Holy Royal Arch Degree
I renounce oaths taken and curses involved in the Holy Royal Arch Degree. I renounce the oath regarding the removal of the head from the body and the exposing of the brains to the hot sun. I renounce the false secret name of God, JAHBULON, and the secret password AMMI RUHAMAH, and all they mean. I renounce the false communion or Eucharist taken in this degree. I renounce all the mockery, skepticism, and unbelief about the redemptive work of Jesus Christ on the cross of Calvary. I renounce the counterfeit rediscovery in the ceremony that takes the candidates through the destruction of King Solomon's Temple, the seventy years of the Babylonian Captivity, and the ultimate return to the Holy Land. I renounce enacting the help, aid, and assistance in the false rebuilding of the City of Jerusalem and the Temple of God. I renounce The Royal Arch or false "Rainbow of Promise" in the ritual. I cut off all these curses and their effects on me and my family, in the name of Jesus Christ. I pray for the healing of my brain, and my mind, in Jesus' name, amen.

Council of Royal Master Degree and Cryptic Rite's Select Master Degree
I renounce oaths taken and curses involved in The Council of Royal Master Degree and The Cryptic Rite's Select Master Degree. I forsake its penalty of having my hands chopped off to the stumps, of having my eyes plucked out from their sockets, and of having my body quartered and thrown among the rubbish of the Temple.

Super Excellent Master Degree and Royal Ark Mariner Degree
I renounce oaths taken and curses involved in the Super Excellent Master Degree and the York Rite's Royal Ark Mariner Degree. I forsake the penalty of having my thumbs cut off, my eyes put out, and my body bound in fetters of brass and conveyed captive to a strange land.

Preceptory of Knights Templar and The Illustrious Order of the Red Cross Degree
I renounce oaths taken and curses involved in The Preceptory of Knights Templar and The Illustrious Order of the Red Cross Degree. I forsake the penalty of having my house torn down and my body being hanged on the exposed timbers.

I renounce the other secret words of KEB RAIOTH and MAHER-SHALAL-HASH-BAZ and all they mean. I renounce the vows taken on a human skull, the crossed swords, and the curse and death wish of Judas. I renounce the curse of having my head cut off and placed on top of a church spire. I renounce the unholy communion and especially drinking from a human skull in many of the York Rites. I repent, renounce, and forsake the entirety of the York Rite, in Jesus' name, amen.

Lodge of Perfection: 4°–14° (Scottish Rite)

The American Lodges conform to the Royal Order of Scotland or The Scottish Rite. Although by 1884, American Albert Pike, radically expanded 4°–33°.

4th or American and Grand Orient Lodges and the Secret Master Degree
I renounce oaths taken and curses involved in the American and Grand Orient Lodges, including the 4th or the Secret Master Degree. I renounce its secret password ADONAI used blasphemously and all its penalties.

5th or Perfect Master Degree
I renounce oaths taken and curses involved in the 5th or Perfect Master Degree and its secret password MAH-HAH-BONE with its penalty of being smitten to the earth with a setting maul. (A wooden instrument used by masons to set polished stone firmly into a wall.)

6th or Confidential Intimate Secretary Degree
I renounce oaths taken and curses involved in the 6th or Confidential Intimate Secretary Degree. I renounce its secret password JEHOVAH used blasphemously and its penalties of having my body dissected, and my vital organs cut into pieces and thrown to the beasts of the field.

7th or Provost and Judge Degree
I renounce oaths taken and curses involved in the 7th or Provost and Judge Degree. I renounce its secret password HIRUM-TITO-CIVI-KY and the penalty of having my nose cut off.

8th or Intendant of the Building Degree
I renounce oaths taken and curses involved in the 8th or Intendant of the Building Degree and its secret password AKAR-JAI-JAH. I renounce the penalty of having my eyes put out, my body cut in two, and exposing my bowels.

9th or Elu or Elected Knights of the Nine Degree
I renounce oaths taken and curses involved in the 9th or Elu or Elected Knights of the Nine Degree. I renounce its secret password NEKAM NAKAH, and its penalty of having my head cut off and stuck on the highest pole in the East.

10th or Illustrious Elect of the Fifteen Degree
I renounce oaths taken and curses involved in the 10th or Illustrious Elect of the Fifteen Degree with its secret password ELIGNAM. I renounce its penalties of having my body opened perpendicularly and horizontally, and my entrails (internal organs) exposed to the air for eight hours so that flies may prey on them, and for my head to be cut off and placed on a high pinnacle.

11th or Sublime Knights Elect of the Twelve Degree
I renounce oaths taken and curses involved in the 11th or Sublime Knights Elect of the Twelve Degree. I renounce its secret password STOLKIN-ADONAI, and its penalty of having my hand cut in twain (two).

12th or Grand Master Architect Degree
I renounce oaths taken and curses involved in the 12th or Grand Master Architect Degree and its secret password RAB-BANAIM and all its penalties.

13th or Knight of the Ninth Arch or Royal Arch of Solomon Degree
I renounce oaths taken and curses involved in the 13th or Knight of the Ninth Arch or Royal Arch of Solomon Degree. I renounce its secret password JEHOVAH used blasphemously and its penalty of having my body given to the beasts of the forest as prey.

14th or Grand Elect, Perfect and Sublime Mason or Perfect Elu Degree
I renounce oaths taken and curses involved in the 14th or Grand Elect, Perfect and Sublime Mason or Perfect Elu Degree. I renounce the secret password, and its penalty of having my body cut open and my bowels given to vultures for food.

Chapter of Rose Croix, 15°–18° (Scottish Rite)

15th or Knights of the East Degree
I renounce the oaths taken and curses involved in the 15th or Knights of the East Degree and its secret password RAPH-O-DOM and its penalties.

16th or Prince of Jerusalem Degree
I renounce oaths taken and curses involved in the 16th or Prince of Jerusalem Degree. I renounce its secret password TEBET-ADAR and its penalty of being stripped naked and having my heart pierced with a poniard (small, slim dagger).

17th or Knight of the East and West Degree
I renounce oaths taken and curses involved in the 17th or Knight of the East and West Degree, and its secret password ABADDON, and its penalty of incurring the severe wrath of the Almighty Creator of Heaven and Earth.

18th or Most Wise Sovereign Knight of the Pelican and The Eagle and The Sovereign Prince Rose Croix of Heredom Degree
I renounce oaths taken and curses involved in the 18th or Most Wise Sovereign Knight of the Pelican and the Eagle and Sovereign Prince Rose Croix of Heredom Degree. I renounce and reject the Pelican witchcraft spirit, as well as the occult influence of the Rosicrucians and the Kabala in this degree. I renounce the claim that the death of Jesus Christ was a "dire calamity." I renounce the deliberate mockery and twisting of the Christian doctrine of the Atonement. I renounce the blasphemy and rejection of the deity of Jesus Christ, the secret words IGNE NATURA RENOVATUR INTEGRA, and its meaning. I renounce the mockery of the communion taken in this degree, including a biscuit, salt, and white wine. I renounce the 18th Degree, in Jesus' name, amen.

Council of Kadosh, 19°–30° (Scottish Rite)

19th or Grand Pontiff Degree
I renounce oaths taken and curses involved in the 19th or Grand Pontiff Degree, and its secret password EMMANUEL used blasphemously, and all its penalties.

20th or Grand Master of Symbolic Lodges Degree
I renounce oaths taken and curses involved in the 20th or Grand Master of Symbolic Lodges Degree, and it secret password JEKSON-STOLKIN, and all its penalties.

21st or Noachite of Prussian Knight Degree
I renounce oaths taken and curses involved in the 21st or Noachite of Prussian Knight Degree, and its secret password PELEG, and all its penalties.

22nd or Knight of the Royal Axe Degree
I renounce oaths taken and curses involved in the 22nd or Knight of the Royal Axe Degree, and its secret password NOAH-BEZALEEI-SODONIAS, and all its penalties.

23rd or Chief of the Tabernacle Degree
I renounce oaths taken and curses involved in the 23rd or Chief of the Tabernacle Degree, and its secret password URIEL-JEHOVAH, and its penalty that I agree the Earth should open up and engulf me up to my neck so I perish.

24th or Prince of the Tabernacle Degree
I renounce oaths taken and curses involved in the 24th or Prince of the Tabernacle Degree and its penalty that I should be stoned to death and my body left above ground to rot.

25th or Night of the Brazen Serpent Degree
I renounce oaths taken and curses involved in the 25th or Night of the Brazen Serpent Degree, and its secret password MOSES-JOHANNES, and its penalty that I have my heart eaten by venomous serpents.

26th or Prince of Mercy Degree
I renounce oaths taken and curses involved in the 26th or Prince of Mercy Degree. I renounce its secret passwords, GOMEL, JEHOVAH-JACHIN, and its penalty of condemnation and spite by the entire universe.

27th or Knight Commander of the Temple Degree
I renounce oaths taken and curses involved in the 27th or the Knight Commander of the Temple Degree, its secret password SOLOMON, and its penalty of receiving the severest wrath of Almighty God inflicted upon me.

28th or Knight Commander of the Sun or the Prince Adept Degree
I renounce oaths taken and curses involved in the 28th, The Knight Commander of the Sun, or the Prince Adept Degree and its secret password STIBIUM. I renounce its penalties of having my tongue thrust through with a red-hot iron, of having my eyes plucked out, of having my senses of smelling and hearing removed, of having my hands cut off and in that condition to be left for voracious animals to devour me, or executed by lightning from heaven.

29th or Grand Scottish Knight of Saint Andrew Degree
I renounce oaths taken and curses involved in the 29th or Grand Scottish Knight of Saint Andrew Degree, with its secret password NEKAMAH-FURLAC, and its penalties.

30th or Grand Knight Kadosh and Knight of the Black and White Eagle Degree
I renounce oaths taken and curses involved in the 30th or the Grand Knight Kadosh and Knight of the Black and White Eagle Degree. I renounce the secret passwords STIBIUM ALKABAR, PHARASH-KOH, and all they mean. I renounce these degrees, in the name of Jesus. Amen.

Consistory of Sublime Princes, Degrees 31°–32° (Scottish Rite)

31st or Grand Inspector Inquisitor Commander Degree
I renounce oaths taken and curses involved in the 31st, The Grand Inspector Inquisitor Commander Degree. I renounce all the gods and goddesses of Egypt, which are honored in this degree, including Anubis with the jackals' head, Osiris the Sun god, Isis the moon goddess and the sister and wife of Osiris. I renounce the Soul of Cheres, the false symbol of immortality and the chamber of the dead. I renounce the false teaching of reincarnation and the false god RA, the ancient Egyptian creator and solar deity. I renounce the 31st Degree, in the name of Jesus, amen.

32nd or The Sublime Prince of the Royal Secret Degree
I renounce oaths taken and curses involved in the 32nd or Sublime Prince of the Royal Secret Degree. I renounce the secret passwords PHAAL/PARASH-KOL and all they mean. I renounce Masonry's false Trinitarian deity AUM and its three parts: Brahma the creator, Vishnu the preserver, and Shiva the destroyer. I renounce the deity of AHURA MAZDA, the claimed spirit and source of all light, and I renounce the worship with fire, which is an abomination to God. I renounce the drinking from a human skull in this and many rites. I also renounce all other Hindu and Buddhist deities and beliefs, in Jesus' name, amen.

The Grand Sovereign Inspector Degree and The Supreme Council, 33° (Scottish Rite)

33rd or The Grand Sovereign Inspector General Degree and The Supreme Council
I renounce oaths taken and curses involved in the 33rd or The Grand Sovereign Inspector General Degree and The Supreme Council. I renounce the secret passwords, DEMOLAY- HIRUM ABIFF, FREDERICK OF PRUSSIA, MICHA, MACHA, BEALIM, and all they mean; as well as the false use of ADONAI. I renounce all of the former obligations, including of having my tongue torn out by its roots, and all other penalties. I renounce and forsake the declaration that Lucifer is God. I renounce the cable-tow around the neck. I renounce the death wish that the wine drunk from a human skull should turn to poison. I renounce the three infamous assassins of the Grand Master: law, property, and religion. I renounce the greed and witchcraft involved in the attempt to manipulate and control the rest of mankind. I renounce the 33rd Degree, in Jesus' name, amen.

Shriners

I renounce oaths taken and curses involved in the Ancient Arabic Order of the Nobles of the Mystic Shrine or Shriners. I renounce the piercing of the eyeballs with a three-edged blade, the flaying of the feet, the madness, and the worship of the false god Allah as the god of our fathers. I renounce the hoodwink, the mock hanging, the mock beheading, the mock drinking of the blood of the victim, the mock dog urinating on the initiate, and the offering of urine as a commemoration. I renounce Shriners, in Jesus' name, amen.

Objects and Regalia

I will throw away all objects in my possession, which connect me to any and all lodges and occult organizations, including Masonry, Witchcraft and Mormonism. I will rid myself of all regalia, aprons, books of rituals, rings, and other Masonic jewelry. I renounce the compass, the square, the noose, the blindfold, and all other objects of Masonry. I renounce the effects these may have on my family or me. In Jesus' name, amen.

I symbolically remove the blindfold (hoodwink) and give it to the Lord for His disposal. In the same way, I symbolically remove the veil of mourning.

I symbolically cut and remove the noose from around my neck, gather it up with the cable-tow running down my body, and give it all to the Lord for His disposal.

I symbolically remove the chains and bondages of Freemasonry from my body.

I symbolically remove all Freemasonry regalia and armor, especially the Apron.

I symbolically remove the ball and chain from my ankles.

I renounce the false Freemasonry marriage covenant, and I now remove the ring of this false marriage covenant from the 4th finger of the right hand, and I give it to the Lord.

I repent and seek forgiveness for having walked on all unholy ground, including Freemasonry lodges and temples, and any Mormon or other occult organizations.

Closing Prayers

Holy Spirit, I ask that you show me anything else, which I need to do or to pray so that my family and I may be totally free from the consequences of these sins. In the name of Jesus Christ I ask to be delivered from any spirit of sickness, infirmity, and any curse, affliction, addiction, disease, or allergy associated with these sins I have confessed and renounced. I command for Satan and every evil spirit to be loosed from me now, never to return to me or to my family, in Jesus' name, amen.

Father God, I ask humbly for the blood of Jesus Christ, your Son, to sanctify me from all these sins I have confessed and renounced. Please cleanse my spirit, mind, will, emotions, and every part of my body that has been affected by these sins. I now proclaim that Satan and his demons have no legal right to mislead, harm, or manipulate my family or me.

I ask You, Lord, to baptize me in Your Holy Spirit. I rejoice in Your protection as You surround me and fill me with Your Holy Spirit. I enthrone You, Lord Jesus, in my heart, for You are my Lord and my Savior, the source of eternal life. Thank You, Father God, for Your mercy, Your forgiveness, and Your love, in the name of Jesus Christ. Amen.

Additional Lodges Tied to Freemasonry

I renounce oaths taken and curses involved in the following lodges and degrees associated with Freemasonry:

Allied Masonic Degrees
American Knights of Protection (AKP)
Ancient Egyptian Order of Sciots
Ancient Grand Lodge of England (The Ancients) Ancient Mystic Order of Samaritans (AMOS)
Ancient Order of Foresters
Ancient Order of Hibernians

Ancient Order of the Knights of the Mystic Chain Ancient Toltec Rite
Ararat Lodge
Benevolent and Protected Order of Elks (BPOE) Blue Lodge
Buffalos or Ancient Order of Buffalos Cagliostro's Egyptian Rite (Italy/France)
CMA Coming Men of America
Daughters of the Eastern Star (Girls)
Daughters of Isis (DOI)
Daughters of Mokanna
Daughters of the Nile (Women)
Disciples of Memphis
Daughters of Rebekah (Oddfellows) Druids
Eagle Lodge
Elders of Zion
Elks Lodge
Eternal & Universal Brotherhood of Mystics
Fraternal Order of Eagles
French Rite (France, Luxembourg, Greece, Brazil & Louisiana)
Grand College of Rites of the USA
Grand Orient Lodge (France)
Grand Lodge of Ireland
Grand Tilers of Solomon
- Excellent Master Degree
- Masters of Tyre Degree
- Architect Degree
- Grand Architect Degree
- Superintendent Degree

Green Lodge
Grottos of North America
Hermetic Order of the Golden Dawn
High Twelve Club, High Twelve Int'l
Hooded Ladies of the Mystic Den (Women's KKK) Imperial Mystic Legion (IML)
Improved Order of Red Men
Independent Order of Oddfellows
Independent Order of Rechabites
Knight of Constantinople
- Installed Sovereign Master Degree
- Installed Master Degree
- Installed Commander Noah Degree
- Installed Supreme Ruler Degree

Knight Crusader of the Cross
Knights of Malta
Knights of Pythias
Knights of the Red Cross of Constantine Knights of St. Paul
Knights of Templar (Women)

Knights of the York Cross of Honour Ku Klux Klan
Ladies of the Macabees
Ladies Oriental Shrine
Loyal Order of Black Lodges
Loyal Order of Orange Lodges
Loyal Order of Purple Lodges
Manchester Unity Order of Oddfellows
Masonic Royal Order of Germany
Masonic Royal Order of Scotland
    Heredom of Kilwinning Degree
    Knight of the Rosy Cross Degree
Memphis Rite (Paris, Belgium & UK)
Misraim Rite (Original Egyptian)
Moose Lodge
Mormonism
Mystic Order of the Veiled Prophets of the Enchanted Realm National Federated Craft
National Grange
National Sojourners, Inc. (Armed Forces)
Order of the Afrikanische Bauherren (African Architects, Egypt)
Order of Amaranth
Order of the Bath
Order of the Beauceant
Order of the Builders
Order of the Constellations of Jr. Stars Order of DeMolay (Boys)
    Initiatory Degree
    DeMolay Degree
    Degree of Chevalier
Order of Desoms
Orders of the Eastern Star (Women)
    Obedience (Adah) Degree
    Devotion (Ruth) Degree
    Fidelity (Esther) Degree
    Faith (Martha) Degree
    Charity (Electa) Degree
Order of the Golden Chain
Order of Golden Dawn
Order of the Golden Key
Order of the Gold and Rosy Cross (1700's FM Prototype. Germany, Austria, Hungary, N. Italy)
Order of the Good Templars Order of High Priesthood
    Order of High Priesthood Degree
    Order of Melchizadek Degree
Order of Job's Daughters
    First Epoch Degree
    Second Epoch Degree

  Third Epoch Degree
Order of Knight Masons of the U.S.A.
  Knight of Sword
  Knight of the East
  Knight of the East and West
  Installed Chief (Chair Degree)
Order of Malta
Order of Masonic Knights Elus Coens of the Universe Order of Quetzalcoatl or Order of Q
Order of the Rainbow Girls (Ages 12-20)
  Initiation Degree
  Grand Cross of Colors Degree
Order of St. John
Order of St. Lawrence the Martyr Order of St. Thomas of Acon Order of the Scarlet Cord
Order of the Secret Monitor Order of the Serpent
Order of the Silver Trowel
Order of the Temple
Order Templi Orientis or Ordo Templi Orientis (OTO, Aleister Crowley) Order of Thirteen (OT)
Order of The White Shrine of Jerusalem
Philalethes Society
Premier Grand Lodge of England (The Moderns)
Prince Hall Freemasonry (African-American)
Priories of Knights of the York Cross of Honor
Pythian Sisters of the World
Red Branch of Eri
Red Cross of Constantine (RCC)
  Knight of the Red Cross of Constantine Degree
  Knight of the Holy Sepulchre Degree
  Knight of St. John the Evangelist Degree
  Installed Viceroy Degree
  Installed Sovereign Degree
Riders of the Red Robe
Rite Hermetique (France)
Rite Ecossais Philosophique (Paris, 1700's Prototype for all FM)
  4th True Mason Degree
  5th True Mason in the Right Way Degree
  6th Knight of the Golden Key Degree
  7th Knight of the Rainbow Degree
  8th Knight of the Argonauts Degree
  9th Knight of the Golden Fleece Degree
Thrice Illustrious Master
  Order of the Silver Trowel from the Jewel of the Degree
Royal Antediluvian Order of Buffaloes
Royal Ark Mariner
Royal Order of Jesters

Royal Riders of the Red Robe (KKK-Like)
Social Order of Beauceant (Women of Knights Templar) Societas Rosicruciana in Anglia
Societas Rosicruciana in Civitatibus Foederatis (SRICF)
    I Zelator Degree
    II Theoricus Degree
    III Practicus Degree
    IV Philosophus Degree
    V Adeptus Minor Degree
    VI Adeptus Major Degree
    VII Adeptus Exemptus Degree
    VIII Magister Templi Degree
    IX Magus Degree
Society of Blue Friars
Sons of Temperance
Sovereign Order of Knights Preceptor
Sunshine Girls (Pythian Sisters Youth)
Supreme Temple Order of Pythian Sisters
Swedish Rite (Sweden, Norway, Iceland, Denmark & Finland)
    St. John's Degree
    Apprentice
Fellow Craft
Master Mason
    St. Andrew's Degree
    Elect & Very Worshipful Scottish Apprentice & Fellow
    Enlightened Scottish Master of St. Andrew
    Very Illustrious Brother, Knight of the East Chapter Degrees
    Most Illustrious Brother, Knight of the West
    Enlightened Brother of St. John's Lodge
    Knight Commander's Degree
    Most Enlightened Brother
    Knight Commander of the Red Cross
Tall Cedars of Lebanon
Templars of Honor and Temperance
Templar Knights of the KKK
The High Twelve International
United Grand Lodge of England
United Order of the Golden Cross
Woodmen of the World
Ye Ancient Order of the Corks
York Rite Sovereign College of North America

Additional Secret Societies, Fraternities, and Cults
Acacia Fraternity
AKIA (A Klansman I AM)

Aleister Crowley
Alpha Delta
Alpha Delta Gamma
Alpha Phi Alpha
American Legion
B'Nai B'rith
Baden Powell's Scouts
Belmont Brotherhood
Bilderberg Club or Group
Bohemian Club at Bohemian Grove Brotherhood of Electrical Employees (Secret)
Chi Omega (Women's Sorority)
Children of the American Revolution
Circle of Honor
Court of Honor
Daughters of the American Revolution
Delta Phi Kappa
DKE (Delta Kappa Epsilon)
Friars Chapter of Mortar Board
Illuminati
IMP Society
Independent International Order of Owls Knights of Columbus (Catholic)
LSV Society
Missouri Paw Paw Militia
Mormonism
Mystic Brothers
Mystic Order of Eli Banana
Mystic Seven (Secret Society)
New Order of Knights NOK (KKK)
Omicron Delta Kappa (ODK)
Order of Owls (OOO)
Order of Skull and Bones
P.E.O. Sisterhood
P.U.M.P.K.I.N., the Sons and Daughters of Liberty Phi Beta Kappa (William & Mary College)
Phi Sigma
Princes of Syracuse
QEBH Society
Rite of Memphiz and Mitzraim
Rollins Society
Round Table
Scroll & Key Society
Select Knights of America
Seven Society
Sigma Gamma Chi
Sigma Mu Sigma

Sigma Sigma Sigma (Women's Sorority)
Sons of the American Legion
T.I.L.K.A
Tau Kappa Epsilon
The 21 Society
The A.N.G.E.L.S. Society
The Boule (a black Greek secret society); The Priory of Sion
The Purple Shadows
The Sons of Liberty
Theta Rho (Odd Fellows)
Thule Society
Z Society

PRAYER FOR BREAKING THE POWER OF WITCHCRAFT[2]

(Those who qualify for the Freemasonry prayer are also in need of this prayer to break witchcraft.)

Heavenly Father, I love you, and I will serve you and you alone. I declare that Satan's control in my life is over, and his assignments are broken, in Jesus' name. I repent and renounce all contact with witchcraft and the occult, willingly or in ignorance, known or unknown.

I repent and renounce of all contact with witchcraft and the occult by my ancestors to the third, fourth, tenth generation and beyond.

I repent and renounce and break all power I have received from any and all involvement with witchcraft and the occult. I break all agreements, all pacts, all contracts, and all deals made with Satan.

In Jesus' mighty name and by the power of His shed Blood, I repent and renounce all involvement with Ouija boards, Magic-8 ball, séances, astrology, horoscopes, fortune telling, ESP. I repent of and renounce all involvement with palm readers, tarot cards, all psychic readings, the 3rd eye, levitation, communication with the dead, all forms of deception, control and manipulation, and rebellion.

I repent and renounce all involvement with black magic, white magic, yoga, meditations, crystals, runes, fetishes, and automatic handwriting. I break all chants, spells, vows, covenants, and incantations, including the effects of all Freemasonry.

I renounce all sacrifices, including blood sacrifices, both animal or human; I break all blood oaths and blood vows.

Notes

[1] Adapted from "Prayer of Release for Freemasons and Their Descendants," Selwyn Stevens Ph.D., *Unmasking Freemasonry—Removing the Hoodwink* (Wellington, New Zealand: Jubilee Resources International Inc.). www.jubileeresources.org. Used by permission.

[2] Reprinted from *Deliverance Training Manual*, William Sudduth and Judith Sudduth (Stephens City, VA: RAM Inc., 2000). Used by permission.

"It's here at last—a scripturally rich, spiritually grounded, practical handbook on deliverance ministry and spiritual warfare. My own heart was encouraged to see greater spiritual advances after reading this book."

–Dr. Michael L. Brown, PhD

Look for the companion book by Stephen Beauchamp:

Power to Deliver: A Guide to Spiritual Warfare and Freedom
ISBN: 978-0-7684-0716-7

For additional resources from Stephen Beauchamp visit
stephenbeauchamp.org

International House of Prayer
INTERNSHIPS

INTRO TO IHOPKC • FIRE IN THE NIGHT
ONE THING INTERNSHIP • SIMEON COMPANY

ihopkc.org/internships

Internships exist to see people equipped with the Word of God, ministering in the power of the Holy Spirit, engaged in intercession, and committed to outreach and service.

Our four internships are three to six months long and accommodate all seasons of life. The purpose of the internships is to further prepare individuals of all ages as intercessors, worshipers, messengers, singers, and musicians for the work of the kingdom. While each internship has a distinctive age limit, length, and schedule, they all share the same central training components: corporate prayer and worship meetings, classroom instruction, practical ministry experience, outreach, and relationship-building.

Biblical teaching in all of the internships focuses on intimacy with Jesus, ministry in the power of the Holy Spirit, the forerunner ministry, evangelizing the lost, justice, and outreach. Interns also receive practical, hands-on training in the prophetic and healing ministries.

Upon successful completion of a six-month internship or two three-month tracks, some will stay and apply to join IHOPKC staff.

Our IHOPKC Leadership Team

Our leadership team of over a hundred and fifty men and women, with diversity of experience, background, and training, represents twenty countries and thirty denominations and oversees eighty-five departments on our missions base. With a breadth of experience in pastoral ministry, missions work, education, and the marketplace, this team's training in various disciplines includes over forty master's degrees and ten doctorates.

International House of Prayer Missions Base, 3535 E. Red Bridge Road, Kansas City, MO 64137
(816) 763-0200 | internships@ihopkc.org

MIKE BICKLE
TEACHING LIBRARY

Free Teaching & Resource Library

This International House of Prayer resource library, encompassing more than thirty years of Mike's teaching ministry, provides access to hundreds of resources in various formats, including streaming video, downloadable video, and audio, accompanied by study notes and transcripts, absolutely free of charge.

You will find some of Mike's most requested titles, including *The Gospel of Grace*; *The First Commandment*; *Jesus, Our Magnificent Obsession*; *Romans: Theology of Holy Passion*; *The Sermon on the Mount: The Kingdom Lifestyle*; and much more.

We encourage you to freely copy any of these teachings to share with others or use in any way: "our copyright is the right to copy." Older messages are being prepared and uploaded from Mike's teaching archives, and all new teachings are added immediately.

Visit mikebickle.org

International House of Prayer Missions Base, 3535 E. Red Bridge Road, Kansas City, MO 64137
(816) 763-0200 | info@ihopkc.org | ihopkc.org